(7)

Differentiated
Staffing

Differentiated Staffing: A Flexible Instructional Organization

A. JOHN FIORINO
TEMPLE UNIVERSITY

Harper & Row, Publishers
New York, Evanston, San Francisco, London

72-12766

Dedication
To Mary, Mary Ann, and Michael

Contents

Preface

The 1960s and 1970s are sure to be recorded by educational historians as the "Age of Innovation." We have seen non-graded schools, team teaching, performance contracting, programmed instruction, computer-assigned instruction, ETV, the middle school, and numerous other innovative ideas proposed and adopted as possible solutions for educational ills. While many innovative ideas were proposed in the last decade, few have lived up to their advanced billing. This unfortunate situation appears to have been caused by, among other factors, exaggerated claims for the idea and/or inadequate preparation for implementation. ETV is an excellent example of an innovation that was oversold. The early proponents of ETV made it sound as miraculous as the old patent medicines of yesteryear. It seemed that the only claim not made for ETV was that it would insure a winning football team—although some may have suggested that it might help.

The "core curriculum," on the other hand, never lived up to its potential largely due to inadequate preparation for implementation. Teachers either volunteered or, as more often happened, were assigned to teach core classes. Unfortunately, few of these teachers were prepared to cope with the demands made by an interdisciplinary course. The typical combination of history and English taught during a double period usually resulted in a teacher teaching history during one period and English the other period. This resulted in frustration and eventual abandonment of the core curriculum. Experience has proven that the concept of a core curriculum is a viable curricular mode. We now see an increasing number of school districts adopting an interdisciplinary approach to curricular organization. The adoption of humanities courses is indicative of the potential of the core curriculum. If appropriate preparations had been made for the implementation of core, we would now have had approximately two decades of experience with interdisciplinary courses.

A recent entry in the field of innovative education has been the differentiation of teaching roles. Differentiated staffing, as it is being called, is based on the notion that students are not the sole possessors of individual differences. Teachers also differ in their needs, desires, knowledges, and skills. We seem to have gone beyond the day when all elementary teachers are thought of as alike. The growing complexity of life—subject matter, skills, instructional materials and media —and the teaching-learning act, with a wide variety of instructional and learning modes, has placed a severe strain on the classroom teacher who attempts to cope with these new and complicated developments. The differentiation of staff tasks and functions is being suggested by many educators as a means for coming to terms with and alleviating the problems created by the new knowledge and awarenesses generated during the past two decades. After careful study and involvement, many educators are convinced that differentiated staffing is worthy of consideration, but they are concerned that it may become a victim of some of the pitfalls mentioned earlier—hence, the purpose of this book.

First, no exaggerated claims are made for differentiated staffing. It cannot be viewed as a panacea which will solve all of the staffing and instructional problems faced by school districts across the country. The first purpose of this book is to provide the reader with a background of information that will allow him to make a rational rather than visceral judgment of the applicability of differentiated staffing. Each educator and school district must decide whether or not differentiated staffing is the answer for them.

While making the determination of the viability of differentiated staffing for a school district, each educator must recognize that a move to differentiated staffing will affect virtually the total school district. Curriculum, instruction, scheduling, space utilization, staff roles and responsibilities, administration and supervision will all be affected. The move to staff differentiation must be viewed as a means to improve the educational opportunities for the clients of the system— the students. It is for this reason that the title, *Differentiated Staffing: A Flexible Instructional Organization,* was selected. Differentiated staffing is viewed as a means to upgrade the quality of instruction and learning through "flexible instructional organization" or FIO which will allow for more individualized learning programs for students.

Second, the need for adequate preparation prior to the adoption of differentiated staffing cannot be overemphasized. The fact that every facet of the educational process within a school district will be affected demands that diligent, comprehensive, and systematic planning must precede the implementation of any FIO model. In addition, the assumption is made that when dealing with individuals there is no "best" way to do anything in education because we are dealing with individual differences. Unfortunately, teachers, as well as students, have individual differences. Therefore, it is concluded that differentiated staffing may not be appropriate for all school districts; that, where deemed appropriate, a staffing pattern and method of operation must be tailor-made to compensate for the uniqueness of each school district. The second purpose, then, is to provide the reader with planning suggestions which will allow for a smooth transition from a traditional staffing pattern to a tailor-made flexible instructional organization.

To accomplish the first purpose, Chapter 1 attempts to provide the rationale for differentiated staffing as much for its proponents as for its critics. Chapter 2 discusses the effect that differentiated staffing models is having on school districts that have implemented their models, and what appear to be emerging trends. A description of three outstanding differentiated staffing models and how they were developed and implemented are included between Chapters 2 and 3.

The remaining chapters are devoted to accomplishing the second purpose: Chapter 3 presents a systems approach to planning and implementing a model; Chapter 4 deals with project management; and Chapter 5 provides suggestions for developing an evaluation and feedback system and procedures for evaluating the model developed in each school district.

Whether or not differentiated staffing will become an accepted and/or viable form of flexible instructional organization will depend on the educators who attempt to implement it. Hopefully, this volume will assist educators' first halting steps in the eventual implementation of an innovative process that will improve the educational opportunities for students and enhance the teaching profession.

A book dealing with innovative ideas is usually handicapped by a lack of practical suggestions that can be utilized by educators. The goal to provide meaningful assistance could not have been achieved without the cooperation of innovative superintendents and staff members. Particular recognition must be given to: Dr. Thomas W. Guilford, formerly Superintendent of Sarasota County Florida Schools, and his successor Gene M. Pillot; Dr. M. John Rand, Superintendent of Temple City California Unified School District, and Staff Member Michael Stover; and Dr. George N. Smith, Superintendent of Mesa Arizona Public Schools, former Project Director Fenwick W. English (now with the Sarasota County Schools), and Associate Director James K. Zaharis. They all provided a great deal of time and valuable assistance in preparing the model reports, and on behalf of myself and the practicing educators who will benefit from having the models available, a grateful thank you.

The semicloistered life at a university is not conducive to the types of learning needed to write a book such as this. Many educators working on model development and implementation contributed to my knowledge of conditions in the field. The group is much too large to list, but their willingness to share their ideas and experiences is appreciated.

In any endeavor, certain individuals stand out for their special contributions: Richard Dempsey of the University of Connecticut who introduced me to differentiated staffing; Gene Pillot of the Sarasota County Schools who originated the concept of flexible instructional organization (FIO) and convinced me that it is a more descriptive term than differentiated staffing; and Pat Walker who did exemplary stenographic work. To all these people I wish to express my appreciation.

The warmest gratitude must be conveyed to my wife, Mary, for her support in editing and typing; and to Michael and Mary Ann for being so patient while their father sat in his study writing.

Finally, I am especially indebted to my editor, Lane Akers, for his faith and encouragement.

A.J.F.

Differentiated
Staffing

chapter
one

Differentiated
Staffing as
a Concept

Most of the advocates of differentiated staffing—the theorists as well as those who are working with it—contend that, in one form or another, it must ultimately come. "The pressures being placed upon education to accept more responsibility for the future of society leave no room for comfortable mediocrity," said Dwight Allen, "and the issue is fast becoming a simple one of whether change will be compulsive or rational. It is time to accept our obligation to be rational by building a professional staff organization under which learning can occur by design rather than by accident."[1]

This statement is probably one of the strongest arguments for the need to become familiar with differentiated staffing. Few educators can afford to have differentiated staffing, or for that matter any innovation, forced upon them. Each educator must heed Allen's plea for rational change. The acceptance or rejection of staffing differentiation should be the result of study and rational thought rather than visceral judgment.

[1] *Differentiated Staffing in Schools: Education USA Special Report,* Washington, D.C.: National School Public Relations Association, 1970, p. 9.

Therefore, this chapter will be devoted to a discussion of the concept of differentiated staffing, proposed advantages, and possible disadvantages.

WHAT IS IT?

Any attempt to determine the meaning of the term *differentiated staffing* usually results in the conclusion that it suffers from the "Humpty Dumpty syndrome." When asked what a word meant, Humpty Dumpty replied that it meant whatever he chose it to mean.[2] Although the sources cited here do not fall in this category, such a condition seems to exist today in relation to a definition of differentiated staffing. Roy Edelfeldt suggested,

> Differentiated Staffing is a plan for recruitment, preparation, induction, and continuing education of staff personnel for the schools that would bring a much broader range of manpower to education than is now available. Such arrangements might facilitate individual professional development to prepare for increased expertise and responsibility as teachers, which would lead to increased satisfaction, status, and material reward.[3]

While this definition suggests staffing differentiation, it seems to be more concerned with reasons for adopting differentiated staffing.

Don Barbee appears to strike closer to the heart of the matter in his definition:

> Differentiated Staffing is a concept of organization that seeks to make better use of educational personnel. Teachers and

---

[2] The reference to Humpty Dumpty should not be construed as a criticism of the sources cited here. The term refers to the practice of educators who take concepts developed by innovators and define them in ways to satisfy a particular personal need.

[3] Roy A. Edelfeldt, "Is a Differentiated Staff Worth Risking," *Pennsylvania School Journal,* Vol. 118, No. 2 (December 1969), pp. 103–104.

other educators assume different responsibilities based on carefully prepared definitions of the many teaching functions. The differential assignment of educational personnel goes beyond traditional staff allocations based on common subject matter distinctions and grade level arrangements and seeks new ways of analyzing essential teaching tasks and creative means of "implementing new educational roles."[4]

The question "What is differentiated staffing?" was given a straightforward answer in a lead article in the *Nation's Schools:*

There is no precise definition, but it implies a restructuring and redeployment of teaching personnel in a way that makes optimum use of their talents, interests, and commitments, and affords them greater autonomy in determining their own professional development. A fully differentiated staff includes classroom teachers at various responsibility levels and pay—assigned on the basis of training, competence, educational goals, and difficulty of task—subject specialists, special service personnel, administrative and/or curriculum development personnel (who may also teach a percentage of their time), and a greater number of subprofessionals and nonprofessionals, such as teaching interns and teacher aides.[5]

The definitions presented here demonstrate an obvious development and explication of the concept. Four fundamental characteristics of differentiated staffing are either mentioned or implied in each of the definitions. First, the staff will be differentiated by the tasks and functions they perform rather than by subject or grade level. Second, a hierarchy will be established which will have several salary levels. Third, cate-

---

[4] Don Barbee, "Differentiated Staffing: Expectations and Pitfalls," *TEPS Write-in Paper No. 1 on Flexible Staffing Patterns,* Washington, D.C.: National Council on Teacher Education and Professional Standards, March 1969, p. 2.
[5] "Differentiated Staffing," *Nation's Schools,* Vol. 85, No. 6 (June 1970), p. 43.

gories in the hierarchy will be determined by the type and/or degree of responsibility assigned to each position. Fourth, regardless of the placement of a position on the hierarchy, all positions will retain some degree of involvement in the instructional process. These characteristics of differentiated staffing substantiate the claim that a sharp break with traditional staffing patterns and procedures is required. Although a distinct change may be called for, the break may not be as clean-cut as it first appears.

DEVELOPMENT OF DIFFERENTIATED STAFFING

The only distinguishing feature of the differentiated-staffing movement appears to be the degree of change proposed. Traditionally, proposals for staffing changes have involved a relatively minor change in the existing staff. An example is the establishment of the position of curriculum coordinator. The advocates of differentiated staffing have taken the position that this type of piecemeal adaptation has not significantly improved the educative process. They have concluded, perhaps rightly so, that the only way to improve education is to make a drastic change in the formula for utilization of staff; but, as a concept, staffing differentiation is not new.

The first differentiation of staff probably occurred when it was decided that one of the teachers in a school should be designated as principal-teacher and was assigned certain responsibilities not usually associated with teaching. Since that time, countless other positions that differentiated functions have been created. The modern school district has any number of staff members performing specialized functions. The interesting factor associated with this development is that the differentiation has occurred in the administrative and special-service areas. The instructional staff has been affected very little by these developments.

Although the present proposals to differentiate instructional functions and tasks may appear to have burst upon the scene in the last few years, the beginnings can be traced to the Committee on the Experimental Study of the Utilization of the Staff in the Secondary School, which sponsored experimentation in 1956. These experiments touched on such areas as *team teaching,* large- and small-group instruction, independent study, the employment of teacher assistants, and the use of technological devices in new and daring ways. J. Lloyd Trump[6] organized the results of these studies and proposed what has become known as team teaching.

Following closely on the heels of team teaching, Myron Lieberman[7] proposed a hierarchy of sorts. Using the medical model, he described an elementary school staffed by three teachers with doctorates and 17 with bachelor's degrees. The teachers holding doctorates were the "doctors," and those holding bachelor's degrees were "nurses." Lieberman cited these advantages for his plan:

1. The school would have persons with high technical competence on the staff.
2. In-service education could be conducted on the scene.
3. Teacher turnover would occur primarily at the "nurse" level.
4. The plan would not raise costs because not all personnel in the hierarchy would have to be paid "professional" salaries.

As will be seen shortly, similar advantages are claimed for the current differentiated staffing plan.

The concept of differentiated staffing as it is proposed today was given its final impetus by Dwight Allen. The fa-

[6] J. Lloyd Trump and Dorsey Baynham, *Focus on Change—Guide to Better Schools,* Skokie, Ill.: Rand McNally, 1961, 147 pp.

[7] Myron Lieberman, *The Future of Public Education,* Chicago: University of Chicago Press, 1960, pp. 95–100.

miliar four-step hierarchy and differentiations by function were probably the most significant contributions that Allen made to the present-day concept. Improvements and refinements are continually being added as school districts develop and implement new differentiated staffing models. This evolution can be seen in the models described following Chapter 2. With all the activity in model development found around the country, the question of cause arises. Perhaps the reason can be found in the rationale being proposed for differentiated staffing.

RATIONALE FOR DIFFERENTIATED STAFFING

Traditional staffing patterns and the role expectation for teachers have been strained to the point of failure by an increasingly complex society and technology. This can be seen in the high dropout rate among beginning teachers and the increasing public dissatisfaction with the education being provided for students. Proponents of differentiated staffing suggest that the cause of these problems centers on the almost impossible situation in which teachers find themselves. A beginning teacher is expected to assume the same responsibilities as a 25-year veteran. In addition, the teacher is expected to be, among other things, a scholar, tutor, instructional strategist, curriculum planner, lesson planner, technologist, child psychologist, diagnostician, and counselor. Few individuals can function adequately in all these roles.

The advocates of differentiated staffing suggest that staff differentiation can overcome these problems. An instructional hierarchy based on differentiation by function and responsibility provides many advantages over the traditional staffing pattern. The individual differences of teachers are recognized, as those of children are. This means that the strengths of teachers can be more effectively utilized in the teaching-learning process. Under this system teachers will no longer have to feel frustration because they cannot fill the role of the omnicapable person. Further, many of the clerical and routine tasks that have perennially plagued teachers will be performed by paraprofessionals or aides. Teachers can then concentrate on tasks directly related to teaching and learning.

The new staffing pattern, with extensive use of paraprofessionals, allows for the individualization of instruction. Two characteristics of differentiated staffing would make this sought-after goal achievable. First, the utilization of paraprofessionals and aides will free teachers to work with individual students. Also, as the ratio of adults to children is reduced, the possibilities of working with individual children will increase. Second, if teachers are allowed to perform those tasks and functions which they can perform most effectively, their efficiency should increase. Hence, they will be able to provide assistance to more individual children. A concomitant benefit should be an improvement in the quality of instruction provided the students.

Enhancement of the profession should result from the career ladder provided by the instructional hierarchy. Teachers would no longer have to leave teaching to receive higher salaries. The practice of turning excellent teachers into administrators to reward them will no longer be needed. Teachers desiring more responsibility and a leadership role may satisfy their need by moving up to the next level on the hierarchy. Although this advantage of differentiated staffing is most often cited, another equally beneficial result may accrue. It is reasonable to assume that not all teachers are ready to accept a heavy burden of responsibility or a leadership role. Some teachers, such as housewives, may wish limited involvement in the instructional process. Within the hierarchy, it is possible for a teacher to assume less responsibility than is expected of the regular teacher. In the traditional staffing pattern, a qualified teacher could not be utilized unless she was willing to accept full responsibility for a classroom of children or live with the frustration of serving as a permanent substitute.

Differentiated-staffing enthusiasts also cite the improvement in induction and retention of teachers as another advantage provided by the instructional hierarchy. At the entry level of the hierarchy, the beginning teacher is not expected to assume the same responsibilities as the experienced teacher. During the initial years of teaching, the neophyte teacher is provided with assistance and time to develop the skills which contribute to successful teaching. This time will also provide the instructional staff with an opportunity to determine the potential of each new teacher. Tenure decisions will not have to be made on the basis of rumor or a few isolated visits. The opportunity to grow into the profession coupled with the possibility of advancement in the hierarchy should improve the retention rate of the more capable teachers.

The advantages of differentiated staffing as proposed by its advocates have tended to ignore the profession as a whole. The most distinctive characteristic of teaching is that it is a group profession. Unlike other professions where an individual practitioner is usually responsible for the total service provided the client, the education of a child requires the services of a number of professionals. No one teacher is responsible for the education of an individual or group of children. The traditional staffing pattern, in which all teachers are regarded as the same and placed in individual rooms, has never been successful in providing the coordination needed to supply the appropriate learning experiences in a suitable sequence to promote effective learning. A differentiated staff has the potential of providing the needed coordination. Within the hierarchy are individuals responsible for coordinating the efforts of all the members of the instructional staff, making it possible for them to function as a group.

While the proponents of differentiated staffing have been busy extolling its virtues, the critics have been equally busy. Experience indicates that no new idea is without fault. Therefore, in the name of justice, the critics should be heard.

CRITICISMS AND PROBLEMS

The charge most often hurled at the advocates of differentiated staffing is that their innovation is nothing more nor less than merit pay in disguise. Few terms upset teachers more than *merit pay,* but this accusation cannot be dismissed too lightly. A clear distinction is made by the proponents between merit pay and the hierarchical salary schedules which are part of all differentiated staffing models. Merit pay is used as a means of rewarding teachers who have demonstrated exceptional achievement in the performance of their duties. The salaries paid to the instructional staff that is differentiated has no relationship to achievement or effectiveness. The determination of salary is based on the amount and nature of responsibility associated with a given position. Hence, the more responsibility a person is willing to accept, the more salary he is paid. Simply stated, merit pay is determined by effectiveness and differentiated pay is determined by responsibility. A logical conclusion that might be drawn is that the parallel with merit pay is being used as an emotional issue aimed at preventing rational consideration of the feasibility of differentiated staffing. There are more worthwhile criticisms than merit pay to occupy the minds of serious educators.

Some critics have suggested that differentiated staffing may lead to overspecialization. This criticism merits serious study by any school district contemplating a move to differentiated staffing. Careful consideration must be given to the effect that overspecialization might have on the social and emotional development of children. The medical model of group practice appears to have limited application to education because a group of doctors has limited contact with large segments of the population, and their services are normally limited to a relatively small aspect of the total life of the patient. If the frustration expressed by many people about the overspecialization of doctors is any indication of what might be expected in education, great caution must be used in developing a differentiated-staffing model. The only defense of staffing differentiation which appears plausible is that there is no intrinsic quality of differentiated staffing that will cause overspecialization. The model designed by any school district should reflect the concerns of a majority of the school staff. The developers of differentiated-staffing models should keep in mind that overspecialization is a possibility and make every effort to come to terms with this potential problem. Perhaps the model planners could state as one of their objectives the maintenance of some generalist capabilities for all members of the staff.

The charge that new roles are being expected of teachers but comparable changes are not demanded of administrators has also been made by opponents of differentiated staffing. As was cited above, there is nothing in the concept of differentiated staffing that would cause this situation to exist. To the contrary, the experience of numerous school districts suggests that the role of the administrator has changed drastically as differentiated staffing models have been implemented. The report dealing with the Temple City model, given following Chapter 2, indicates that the administrators probably had to make more adjustments to their new roles than did the teachers. Clearly, this criticism can be taken into account during the planning process.

Cost is an important consideration in the operation of any school district. The suggestion has been made that staff differentiation will substantially increase the per-pupil cost of educating the children in a school district. Here again, experience shows that differentiated staffing need not increase costs greatly. Temple City handled this problem by stating that no model would be acceptable unless it could be funded by existing budget constraints. After several attempts, a model was developed which satisfied this requirement. The report of the Sarasota County model (following Chapter 2) provides a comparison of the actual cost of the traditional and differentiated staffing patterns. The result of this comparison demonstrates that the increase in cost amounted to approximately 1 percent, but the slight increase provided benefits not available in the traditional staffing pattern.

Time is also a valuable commodity in the educative process. Some critics have pointed out that an inordinate amount of time is needed for planning and coordination of the instructional process. Both theory and practice designate planning and coordination time as important ingredients that will enhance the effectiveness of a differentiated staff. The advocates of differentiated staffing justify the expenditure of this time in two ways. First, it is pointed out that the utilization of paraprofessionals and aides provides time for staff planning without depriving the students of needed guidance and supervision. Second, the quality of contact with students is emphasized rather than the quantity. If a portion of the time a teacher spends with students can be categorized as "glorified baby-sitting," then the amount of time a teacher spends with students becomes an almost meaningless concern. The most significant dimension of the teaching-learning act is the effectiveness of the teacher. Consequently, time spent in planning and coordination should significantly contribute to quality of teaching.

Any new idea invites the criticism that it is new and untested, and hence, should be avoided. The fact that differentiated staffing is relatively new has contributed to the position taken in this book that it may not be appropriate for all school districts at this time. Many questions remain to be answered. Even some of the strongest supporters of differentiated staffing seldom give unqualified support. Florida Superintendent of Instruction Floyd T. Christian, a strong supporter, has said:

> Differentiated staffing is *one emerging educational plan* which purports to have significant advantages for improving the traditional system of school organization and should remain highly exploratory. Dramatic action should be taken without delay to understand the implications of this concept before unqualified endorsements are made.[8]

At this stage in the development of the differentiated-staffing concept, there is a clear need to have it tested by school districts that recognize its limitations and possible pitfalls. Any school district attempting to implement a differentiated-staffing model should start with the assumption that it is engaging in an experimental effort to determine the feasibility of the concept. In this way, the data needed for evaluating the viability of differentiated staffing will be available to the majority of school districts in the country. The most disastrous development would be to have school districts view differentiated staffing as an excellent attention-getting novelty. If this should occur, differentiated staffing will join the other "abandoned bandwagons" at the side of the road to quality education.

The remainder of this book is devoted to assisting sincere educators as they consider the possibilities of staffing differ-

[8] Floyd T. Christian, *State Commissioner Speaks on Flexible Staff Utilization: A Position Statement on the Concept of Differentiated Staffing*, Tallahassee, Florida: Department of Education, 1969, p. 7.

entiation and prepare to implement a differentiated-staffing model. In addition, it should demonstrate to the uncommitted educator the amount of effort and commitment needed to plan a reasonably successful model.

SUMMARY

Differentiated staffing is a concept which proposes to improve the effectiveness of instructional staff personnel by capitalizing on their strengths. Its four characteristics include:

1. Differentiation by functions and responsibilities
2. A hierarchy of several salary levels
3. Type and/or degree of responsibility determining placement in the hierarchy
4. Involvement of all positions in the instructional process

Although it is viewed as a recent development, the roots of differentiated staffing can be traced back to the staff utilization studies sponsored by the National Association of Secondary School Principals.

Some of the advantages attributed to differentiated staffing by its proponents are the following:

1. It capitalizes on the individual differences found in teachers.
2. It improves conditions for providing individualized instruction.
3. It provides a career ladder for the instructional staff.
4. It enhances the induction and retention of teachers.
5. It allows for better coordination of instructional activities.

Opponents of differentiated staffing suggest:

1. It is really merit pay in disguise.
2. Overspecialization will result.
3. New demands are made of teachers but not administrators.
4. It will raise the cost of educating students.

5. Excessive planning time will be needed.
6. It has not been tested and proven.
7. It is an attention-getting novelty.

Each of these criticisms was carefully considered and the conclusion was drawn that, although adequate data is lacking to make a confident prediction, the concept of differentiated staffing deserves study and experimental implementation.

SELECTED BIBLIOGRAPHY

Allen, Dwight W. "A Differentiated Staff: Putting Teaching Talent to Work." *The Teacher and His Staff, Occasional Papers No. 1.* Washington, D.C.: National Commission on Teacher Education and Professional Standards, National Education Association (December 1967), 12 pp.

Connors, Joy. "Building a Career Ladder." *American Education,* 5: 15–17 (February 1969).

Edelfelt, Roy A. *Redesigning the Education Profession.* Washington, D.C.: National Commission on Teacher Education and Professional Standards, National Education Association (January 1969), 17 pp.

English, Fenwick. "Differentiated Staff: Education's Technostructure." *Educational Technology, 10:* 24–27 (February 1970).

English, Fenwick. "Teacher May I? Take Three Giant Steps! The Differentiated Staff." *Phi Delta Kappan, 51:* 211–214 (December 1969).

Joyce, Bruce R. *The Teacher and His Staff: Man, Media, and Machines.* Washington, D.C.: National Commission on Teacher Education and Professional Standards, and Center for the Study of Instruction, National Education Association (1967), 28 pp.

Lierheimer, Alvin P. "An Anchor to Windward." *TEPS Write-in Papers on Flexible Staffing Patterns No. 2.* Washington, D.C.: National Commission on Teacher Education and Professional Standards, National Education Association (April 1969).

National Education Association, National Commission on

Teacher Education and Professional Standards. *A Position Paper on the Concept of Differentiated Staffing.* Washington, D.C.: The Commission (1969), 7 pp.

National Education Association, National Commission on Teacher Education and Professional Standards. *The Teacher and His Staff: Differentiating Teaching Roles.* Report of the 1968 Regional TEPS Conferences. Washington, D.C.: The Commission (1969), 120 pp.

Rand, M. John and Fenwick W. English, "Towards a Differentiated Teaching Staff." *Phi Delta Kappan, 40:* 264–268 (January 1968).

chapter two

Differentiated Staffing in Practice

A college administrator often reminds the members of his faculty that ideas are as common as dirt and that we have more ideas than we can use. He points out that what is needed is people who can implement some of the more promising ideas that already exist. Whether we have an excess of ideas may be debatable, but the need for implementing promising ideas can hardly be disputed. The most challenging task in education seems to be the implementation of ideas so that they prove to be as advantageous in practice as they seem in theory. In the previous chapter, the ideas of the theorists and proponents of differentiated staffing were presented. Now the question is "How have the practitioners in the field implemented these ideas?"

At this point in time, a limited amount of data is available. Approximately thirty school districts throughout the country have received funding to plan and implement differentiated staffing models. Of this number, only five have two or more years experience with planning and implementation. Two of the five have been included in the models following Chapter 2. Therefore, no attempt will be made in this chapter to present a critique of the various projects. Instead, an analysis will be made of what appear to be common elements in the various models and the effect that staffing differentiation seems to be having on organization and administration and the educative process.

COMMON ELEMENTS OF MODELS

The most common element found in all the differentiated staffing models is the hierarchy for the instructional staff. As might be expected, the number of levels in the hierarchy varies from district to district. They range from three to seven, depending on whether paraprofessionals and aides are included with professional staff members. Four levels appear to be most prevalent for members of the professional staff.

Level-One Teachers

The lowest level in the hierarchy is almost universally viewed as the entry level for beginning teachers. Some model developers also perceive this level as an excellent position for experienced teachers who, for various personal reasons or obligations, prefer a limited involvement in the total educative process. The primary functions and tasks of teachers at this first level usually are restricted to the execution of curricular and instructional plans prepared by staff members at higher levels in the hierarchy. Not only do the teachers at this level devote all their time to instruction, but their involvement—particularly that of beginning teachers—is limited. A teacher at this level would:

1. Work with homogenous groups of children
2. Not be given diagnostic responsibility
3. Function, in many instances, as a junior member of a team
4. Be provided a work load which would allow for a relatively smooth induction into the profession

A common practice appears to be to assign a teacher to this level for a probationary period lasting from three to four years. Normally, tenure is not given for this rank unless it is conceived as a career level with an appropriate salary schedule. In either case, promotion to the next rank is not automatic. Obviously, teachers at this level are not required to accept the wide range of responsibilities that the experienced teachers must assume.

Level-Two Teachers

The teacher at the second level is comparable to the traditional classroom teacher but has proven the ability to accept a wide range of responsibilities. In addition to the accepted tasks associated with teaching, this teacher would:

1. Work with groups of students having heterogenous abilities
2. Participate in curriculum-development activities
3. Assist in staff-evaluation process
4. Provide guidance to level-one staff members
5. Function as a team member or individual teacher
6. Assist in or plan for instruction
7. Accept responsibility for a given group of students

Generally speaking, the teachers at level two—often called staff teachers—form a cadre of experienced teachers who do not desire additional responsibilities. They have the experience and flexibility to be utilized in a variety of situations. It has been suggested that the staff, or level-two, teachers are the backbone of the school. In most models, they would constitute the largest group of professionals.

Level-Three Teachers

The third-level teacher, often called senior or directing teacher, will probably be viewed as a new staff member by proponents of differentiated staffing and as a supervisor by critics. While a cursory examination may suggest a similarity to the traditional supervisor, a close study of the position reveals that the two are not analogous. The first and most obvious difference is that the teacher at this level has instructional responsibility on a regular basis. In addition to teaching part-time, the functions and tasks of the senior teacher might include:

1. Devising new teaching strategies for implementing curricular plans
2. Diagnosing learning problems and prescribing remedial activities
3. Serving as an advisor in curriculum development and research projects
4. Coordinating the work of all teachers in a given subject or skill area
5. Serving as a team leader
6. Assuming responsibility for selection, training, performance, and evaluation of paraprofessionals in his area
7. Assisting in discovering and refining methods for working with individuals
8. Conducting or arranging for in-service classes, workshops, and seminars for teachers, dealing with methods and techniques in skill and subject areas

The teacher occupying this position may be the leader of a team, a grade level, or a department, and probably has a line or direct authority rather than staff or consultive authority position. This person would be accountable for a limited part of the instructional program.

Level-Four Teachers

Consulting or master teacher and instructional coordinator are some of the titles given to teachers who occupy the highest position in the instructional hierarchy. The teacher at this level has the broadest range of responsibility that is directly rooted in classroom teaching. The hallmark of this position is leadership in a broad area of the instructional program. He may be responsible for coordinating several grade levels, or several disciplines in a school or grade level. There appears to be no definite preference in the matter of authority. Both line and staff authority have been assigned to this position, but, generally, this person provides developmental, consultative, and advisory services. Some of his specific functions might be to:

1. Provide leadership in designing experimental instructional projects based on research
2. Maintain a liaison with universities, research centers, industry, and business
3. Manage curriculum-development activities for his area of responsibility
4. Conduct a continuous program of research and evaluation in his area of responsibility
5. Arrange for and/or conduct in-service classes, workshops, seminars, and discussion groups
6. Prepare proposals for external funding
7. Organize staff to engage in long-range planning
8. Establish, with the instructional staff, curriculum and instructional priorities
9. Develop and maintain a system for the allocation of resources

Obviously, this person would have influence on a large sector of the school population and would perform tasks at a level of sophistication sufficiently high to require maximum available training and talent. In addition to wide experience and proven ability, the majority of school districts require that the persons occupying this position have an earned doctorate in an area appropriate to their responsibilities. Neither this position nor the level-three position carry tenure. All teachers filling these positions may be granted tenure as teachers at the staff or second level.

Paraprofessionals and Aides

Another common characteristic of the various differen-tiated-staffing models is the extensive use of *paraprofessionals* and *aides*. A clarification of terms may be helpful prior to a discussion of roles. A paraprofessional is usually, but not always, a person with some college background and skills not usually associated with the average layman. These are people who do not require close supervision but are not expected to make professional judgments. A library assistant, theme reader, or instructional assistant could be classified as a para-professional. They may have received training on the job or at one of the increasing number of community colleges which have programs for preparing instructional assistants. An aide is normally assigned duties which are primarily clerical, technical, or monitorial.

The titles given the subprofessional levels vary greatly, but there appear to be three basic categories. The first is the instructional assistant, who usually works with one or more staff teachers. They are utilized in various follow-up activities, tutoring individual students, proctoring examinations, obtain-ing and organizing instructional materials, preparing visual aids, and other activities related to the instructional process. In no case are instructional assistants expected to perform duties which require an interpretation or adaptation of the instructional program.

The general classification aide is the second category of subprofessional. Laymen and both high school and college students are normally utilized as aides. They perform many of the clerical tasks associated with teaching. These include typ-ing, recording test scores, duplicating materials, taking attend-ance, collecting money, and the countless other clerical tasks associated with teaching. In addition, they may be used to assist in such noninstructional situations as the supervision of groups of students during lunch, recess, or the loading and unloading of buses. In some schools, aides are allowed, under close supervision, to work with individual children or small groups.

The third category includes laymen who have specialized vocational or avocational skills which allow them to make a special contribution to the instructional program. Sarasota County (Model B following Chapter 2) has assigned the title of *adjunct teacher* to persons in this position. The description of this position in the Sarasota County report is an excellent example of how laymen with particular skills are being utilized around the country.

A fourth category, that of *teaching intern,* is used by some school districts but, as yet, is not in common use. The teaching intern is normally a college graduate who is receiving salaried on-the-job experience while in the process of fulfilling certification requirements. In some instances—Beaverton, Oregon, for example—the teaching intern is considered part of the professional staff, and the position is considered a step in the career ladder. This appears to be a promising development, but it is too early to predict future evolution of the position. A closely related development is the utilization of teachers-in-training as interns during their last year of training (see Model B). While this alternative may not be available to many school districts, it is an idea teeming with possibilities. Teacher educators have long proposed the possibility of a 5-year work-study program for preparing teachers. The primary constraint has been the traditional staffing patterns used by school districts. A school district with differentiated staffing would be an ideal setting for utilizing the wide range of abilities in a student body involved in a 5-year work-study program. Both the school district and the college would derive many benefits from cooperating in such an enterprise.

Horizontal Differentiation

Most writing and discussion dealing with staff differentiation is concerned with the vertical or hierarchical dimension, but differentiated staffing also involves various types of specialization at given levels. A teacher may specialize in guiding students on individual projects, work with small discussion groups, or be responsible for large-group instruction. In an elementary school, a team of five teachers might include a reading specialist, a mathematics specialist, a science specialist, and two generalists. The point is that differentiation can be based on the kind or the degree of responsibility that individual teachers accept.

Team Teaching?

A question which invariably arises is "Does differentiated staffing require team teaching?" The answer is that it all depends on how you define team teaching. If team teaching is viewed as a highly structured organization in which a group or team of teachers is responsible for a large group of students, the answer would be that team teaching is not necessary. Conversely, if team teaching is conceptualized as a loose structure which involves close cooperation in implementing curriculum, then the answer would be that team teaching is necessary. In the first situation, the teachers must depend on each other to provide a significant portion of a total program. In the latter situation, an individual teacher may be responsible for the major portion of a total program and utilize other teachers for specialized segments of the program. Either or both structures are possible in a school district which has adopted differentiated staffing.

ORGANIZATION AND ADMINISTRATION

A principle of general systems theory states that changes made in one component or part of a system will affect all other components or parts of the system. Any notion that differentiated staffing is simply a matter of establishing the steps of a career ladder for the instructional staff could not be further from the truth. Principles, whether known or unknown, accepted or rejected, apply in a given situation. This can be seen in the experience of school districts which have implemented staffing differentiation. The impact of the new staffing pattern is noticeable to some degree in all components of the school district. The school as an organization[1] and its administration have been particularly affected.

Decentralized Decision Making

An almost universal effect on schools which have adopted differentiated staffing has been the decentralization of decision making. More decisions, particularly those related to the instructional process, are being made at the "building" or individual school level. Some school districts have organized academic senates in each building. These groups are authorized to make decisions, within general guidelines, which affect them or their students. In Sarasota County, for example, the staff of each school is free, within the stated guidelines, to decide on its own staffing pattern. This means that they can determine the number of staff members they will have at each rank.

The academic senates are also free to determine the teaching-learning strategies that they will use with their students. They may also adapt the curriculum to satisfy the needs of their students, as long as they are working toward achieving the stated objectives. Lip service has been given for years to the concept that school populations, as well as

---

[1] *Organization* is used here to denote a group of people performing specialized functions which contribute to achieving a common goal and governed by formal and informal rules of conduct, rather than in the sense of an ordering as in a table of organization.

individuals, differ. The fact that these differences are being provided for by schools moving to differentiated staffing seems to reinforce the thesis that staff differentiation will effect change throughout the system. In addition, most models provide specified areas in which all members of the staff, regardless of rank, have authority to make decisions. An anathema in most models is the situation in which directives regarding the most inconsequential matters are constantly being communicated from some place on high.

Staff Involvement in Decision Making

An evolving principle in most differentiated-staffing models is that instructional personnel make instructional decisions. This principle, united with the decentralization of decision making, may well prove to be the most potent force in the implementation of a successful differentiated-staffing model. Extensive utilization of instructional personnel in both the planning stages of model development and the ongoing program has been a hallmark of the major differentiated staffing projects. The steering committees formed by the school districts involved in model development to guide the planning process have all had extensive representation from the instructional staff. The task forces organized by the steering committees to plan various aspects of the models have also involved members of the instructional staff. Following implementation of the various models, the school districts have organized a variety of system-wide decision-making groups which include members of the instructional staff. Two types of groups have been organized to deal with general district matters and system-wide curriculum and instruction matters.

Temple City, California (Model A) has established both types of groups. The district senate replaces the traditional administrative council, which was composed of principals, coordinators, directors, and other administrative auxiliary personnel. The voting membership of the senate includes six principals and six members of the instructional staff who are elected by teachers. Ex officio members of the senate include the assistant superintendents—business and personnel directors, coordinators, and master teachers. The functions of the district senate are as follows:

1. To recommend for board approval district policies and programs relating to instruction and curriculum
2. To recommend for board approval support systems needed for instruction, including pupil personnel, media, and evaluation services
3. To develop cooperatively district budget with administrative guidelines and procedures
4. To recommend for board approval district policies and procedures for certificated personnel as they relate to the instructional program
5. To recommend for board approval district policies and procedures relating to classified personnel involved in the instructional program
6. To establish administrative policies and procedures necessary for the implementation of district instructional policies and programs
7. To approve guidelines established by the director of projects with the superintendent
8. To approve district plans and guidelines for transition to differentiated staffing and flexible scheduling
9. To serve as an appellate body in resolving problems submitted by school senates
10. The district senate is responsible to the superintendent for the performance of its duties. The superintendent serves as its executive officer. Where differences occur between the senate and the superintendent, the issue may be appealed to the board of education for joint hearing. In such a hearing all members of the senate, the superintendent,

and the board will participate. The decision of the board will be final.[2]

This statement of functions might well serve as a model for other school districts, but the purpose of including it here is to demonstrate the wide range of areas in which instructional personnel participate in decision making. The most notable feature of the statement is function ten. While many superintendents have practiced this type of administration, few superintendents or school districts have stated in writing that any group within a school district had, in effect, veto power over a superintendent's decision. The suggestion is not being made that all school districts moving to differentiated staffing have included this provision, but virtually all have recognized the need for faculty participation in decision making.

The second group organized by Temple City is the instructional council, which is composed of master teachers (level four) in the various disciplines, the directors of education, and the superintendent. The council is supplemented by discipline-centered vertical committees with senior teacher (level three) representatives from each school, or designates serving in that area, headed by the master teacher. Functions of the instructional council include these:

1. To develop short- and long-term plans for the improvement of curriculum and instruction
2. To recommend to the district senate appropriate support services for the instructional program including pupil personnel and media services
3. To recommend in-service education programs to accomplish instructional goals
4. To conduct annual audits of instructional progress

[2] Fenwick English, *A Handbook of the Temple City Differentiated Staffing Project, 1965–1970*, mimeographed, Temple City Unified School District, 1970, p. 14.

5. To articulate planned sequences of learning in authorized subject areas on K–12 basis
6. To plan and institute with the approval of district senate in-service education programs to prepare staff for transition into differentiated staffing and flexible scheduling
7. To plan for the dissemination of tested practices and programs
8. To effect the district program in curriculum and instruction in keeping with board policies and state law
9. To develop periodic reports to the district senate and the board of education on progress and direction in curriculum and instruction
10. The instructional council is responsible to the district senate for the performance of its duties. The district senate evaluates and approves council proposals which are then effected by the master teacher.[3]

Redefinition of Principal's Role

The increased involvement of teachers in the decision-making process has caused many school districts to examine and redefine the role of the principal. If the instructional staff is to be delegated the authority to make curricular and instructional decisions, what then are the principal's functions? Actually, the only real change which seems to be occurring is that theory and practice are beginning to conform. Theoretically, the principal should spend 50 percent of his time as instructional leader, but for years research has indicated that this ideal was seldom achieved. Principals have perennially been inundated by noncurricular and noninstructional problems and tasks. In a school district utilizing differentiated staffing, the principal need no longer suffer pangs of guilt over neglecting curriculum and instruction. These matters are the primary responsibility of the instructional staff. The principal of a school with differentiated staff would:

[3] *Ibid.*, p. 15.

1. Participate in, but not be responsible for, supervision and evaluation of teachers
2. Assign and supervise work schedules of noninstructional personnel
3. Prepare budget and disburse funds and supplies
4. Communicate and interpret programs to the public
5. Interpret and administer district policy at the building level
6. Interpret and communicate building needs to the central administration and facilitate procedures to meet these needs
7. Communicate with students and act upon their requests and suggestions within district policies

These functions would be the primary responsibility of the principal, but he would also participate in making curricular and instructional decisions. The building academic senate discussed above has the primary responsibility for deciding on the overall policies regarding curriculum and instruction. As a member of the senate, the principal is able to provide inputs into the decision-making process. The only change which seems to have occurred is that the principal no longer has the authority to make the final decision concerning curriculum or instruction. In the event that the principal does not agree with a senate decision, or vice versa, provisions can be made to have the disagreement resolved by the district senate.[4]

THE EDUCATIVE PROCESS

The general systems principle mentioned earlier also applies to the total educative process. It is inconceivable that all the changes discussed to this point would not affect the curriculum or instructional process. In practice what appears to have happened is that curricular and instructional revisions were made before finishing the differentiated-staffing model.

[4] See introduction to Temple City report—Model A following Chapter 2.

This is probably due to the systems approach, to be discussed in the next chapter, which is being used in one form or another by all the funded differentiated-staffing projects. The first step in the systems approach is to determine the objectives of the system. For schools, this means that the objectives of the educational program or curriculum must be stated so that the functions necessary for achieving the objectives can be identified. The basis for differentiation can only be determined when the instructional functions to be performed are known.

Curriculum

The wide variety of possible forms and formats for curriculum preclude a discussion of specific curricula. Therefore, emerging trends will be presented here. Student-centered curriculum appears to be receiving a great deal of attention. Some educators may protest that curriculum has always been student centered, but this position can be seriously questioned. Traditional curriculum is prepared for students and is future-oriented. Students are often told that they will need the things they are learning when they grow up. The proposed student-centered curriculum attempts to deal with problems and questions that students face as they are in the process of growing up. Emphasis is placed on the acquisition of knowledge and development of skills students need to cope with everyday life.

This curricular orientation has led to an emphasis on the development of skills. Another way of describing the evolution that is taking place is to say that the curriculum is process-oriented. For example, science is studied as a process rather than a body of knowledge. The knowledges and principles are not being ignored. They are simply placed in their true perspective as the product of a process engaged in by scientists. Approaching curriculum in this manner appears to provide two very important benefits. It helps the student develop skills which assist him in solving problems he faces, and it contributes to the development of students who are capable of independent learning.

This emphasis on process has influenced the objectives of the curriculum. The first and obvious effect has been on the inclusion of more process or skill objectives. The second effect has been the move toward behavioral- or competency-based objectives. Statements of objectives are written so that they describe the behavior or competency that the student should demonstrate when he has completed a particular unit of instruction. This approach to stating objectives has been challenged on the basis that behavioral objectives ignore the affective dimension of education. This debate can be resolved by avoiding the either-or stance typically taken by educators. It is possible to prepare objectives in two ways. Those which can be stated behaviorally should be so stated, and those which cannot should be stated in such a manner that they are capable of guiding instruction and evaluation. Little can be gained by debating the merits of stating objectives in a particular way.

Giving more emphasis to process and skills has minimized the pressure to include immense amounts of information to fill the school day. An almost universal characteristic of the curricula developed by school districts devising differentiated-staffing models is more variety in the types of learning experiences provided for the students. As the amount of required information is reduced, the possibility for more variety is increased. In addition, the curriculum gains a flexibility which allows for meeting the particular needs of individual students. The curricular changes, in combination with staffing differentiation, have had a profound effect on the instructional process.

Instruction

A hallmark and major purpose of all differentiated-staffing models is individualization of instruction. This can be seen in the curricular changes which make possible individualized learning. As the staff is differentiated, the objective of individualizing instruction is allowed to grow to fruition. This is precisely what has been happening in schools which have differentiated their staffs. While aides are supervising follow-up activities, the teachers are free to work with individual students on problems or projects. The result is that under these conditions a continuous-progress program is possible. There is no need to hold back students because the group they are in has not completed a particular task. Students are able to move as quickly or as slowly as their desire or ability allows.

The only variable not accounted for up to this point is time. The flexibility made possible by the curricular, instructional, and staff changes would be neutralized unless the time allotted for the school day could be used as the need varies. To make this possible, school districts have devised various forms of flexible scheduling. In its Oak Avenue Intermediate School, Temple City has divided the school day into 24 15-minute modules, with 3-minute passing periods. The average class length is 2 modules (33 minutes). Laboratory classes are 3 modules in duration (51 minutes) to allow for the time lost in each session for equipment setup. Classes may meet as often as every day or as infrequently as once a week. Sarasota County has devised what appears to be a very practical and efficient method for providing flexibility in the utilization of time.[5]

Some school districts have also scheduled as much as 40

[5] See Sarasota County report—Model B following Chapter 2.

percent of each upper-grade student's day as unstructured time. The time can be spent on independent study projects, remedial activities, or class projects. Students who are unable or unwilling to use their free time responsibly are given assignments to be completed in a specified room. This approach to teaching and learning requires that the traditional utilization of facilities be revised.

Learning Centers

A *learning center* may be defined as a room where students have free and easy access to purposefully selected materials and equipment, and space to use the materials and equipment while engaged in learning activities. Although this definition may immediately bring to mind a school library, the learning-center concept extends far beyond the traditional library. A more appropriate title might be learning-center laboratory, because what is being proposed is a blend of library and laboratory facilities with space suitable for both individual and group activities. Clearly, any school district which has adopted differentiated staffing and is providing the type of program just described would require the facilities provided by a learning center.

Generally speaking, a learning center would contain books and other printed material. In addition, it would include typewriters, tape recorders and tapes, phonographs and records, filmstrips and viewers, film-loop projectors and single-concept film loops, and, conceivably, a computer terminal. These machines and materials would be common to most learning centers, but the mission of a particular center would determine precisely the type of materials and equipment it contained. As indicated by the practices of many school systems, learning centers can be categorized as general, subject-oriented, motivational, or remedial. The general learning center would normally be a school library augmented by adding the resources mentioned. The curricular needs, financial resources, and creativity of the library and instructional staffs will determine the resources and facilities that will be included in a general learning center. All other types of learning centers tend to be housed in converted classrooms and are staffed by a member of the instructional staff who has the appropriate expertise.

Subject-matter learning centers would contain books and other materials related to the subject emphasis of the center. Such centers would include microscopes, measuring devices, cusinaire rods, meter sticks, maps, globes, plastic models, realia, adding machines, calculators, and games. The list of materials and equipment that might be included in a learning center is almost endless. Any material or equipment which is directly related to or contributes to the ongoing program, can be used for enrichment purposes, or will aid in developing skills associated with a particular subject would be suitable for inclusion.

A motivational learning center would, in most school districts, be found in an elementary school. These centers can be general or subject-oriented, but in either case their purpose is not to teach subject matter or skills per se. A motivational learning center is precisely what the name implies: an environment designed to induce interest in a particular subject or education in general. There would be a tendency to include predominantly sensory materials and facilities, such as puzzles, models, and experimental apparatus, adequate for extensive involvement of students. For such a center to be successful, close cooperation and planning is required of the center staff and classroom teachers, because in the end the classroom teachers must provide follow-up activities to sustain the interest generated by learning centers. A limited number of motivational learning centers are in operation, but interest in them appears to be growing.

The remedial learning center is both an old and new development. It is old in the sense that many schools have set aside a room to use for remedial reading. On the other hand, the developments associated with learning centers have added new dimensions to the old remedial reading room. A remedial learning center is not restricted to students referred to it by teachers, but is available to any student who wishes to overcome a learning handicap or develop a particular study skill. The center is not normally restricted to remediation for a specific area. The emphasis is on general learning disabilities. The staff of a remedial learning center might include a reading specialist, a specialist in general learning disabilities, and an aide. The materials in the center would include diagnostic instruments, self-instruction materials, and materials suitable for use by a teacher with small groups.

The advisability of establishing a remedial learning center or, for that matter, any learning center will depend on need and resources available. The only people in a position to decide on whether a learning center is needed or what type or types should be created are the people who will use it. Consequently, each school district must establish priorities and determine which, if any, of the learning centers mentioned earlier best meets their needs and is within their means.

FLEXIBLE INSTRUCTIONAL ORGANIZATION

Throughout the first two chapters of this book, the terms *differentiated staffing* and *staff differentiation* have been used to describe an innovative idea whose primary purpose was to maximize the effective and efficient utilization of teachers in the instructional process. These terms have been used because they are the most commonly used nationally and, therefore, would be recognized easily. However, as a result of observing implemented models, reviewing the literature in preparation for writing this book, and having many discussions with educators involved in developmental, implementational and ongoing programs, it seems clear that neither of these terms appropriately represents the concept.

These terms have been applied generally to the concept of organizing the instructional staff into a vertical hierarchy and horizontal arrangement to perform those tasks that require the training, experience, ability, and interest possessed by the individual members. The basic purposes of differentiated staffing are to improve the profession by providing a career ladder, involving teachers in decision making that governs the profession, and providing greater satisfaction for teachers by enabling them to perform tasks related to their interests and talents. The ultimate purpose of staff differentiation, however, is to provide for the efficient use of human resources to maximize the quality of education and the individualization of instruction.

Thus, the true *end* is individualized instruction and the *means* is staffing differentiation. The process provides more manpower to diversify and individualize instructional programs and offers alternative modes of participation by teachers and students in the instructional process. This diversification of participation requires flexibility in schedules, class size, group organization, and use of facilities. The word *flexible* applies to all aspects of the instructional program and is a concomitant to staff differentiation. Consequently, adopting a new hierarchy of staff roles without providing the flexibility needed in all other dimensions of the instructional process would present an almost insurmountable obstacle to individualizing instruction. It is suggested, therefore, that the term *differentiated staffing* is an inadequate representation of the principles which are fundamental to the concept of comprehensive flexibility of the instructional program.

The present name may even be a limitation to an understanding of the purpose and promise of differentiated staffing. Many of the criticisms mentioned in Chapter 1 are probably based on the implicit limitation in the differentiation of staff roles. Few educators, however, would argue with the potential benefits of individualizing instruction through the maximum and flexible use of all resources—human, material, spacial, and time. Therefore, if a term more representative of the principles and purposes of differentiated staffing were commonly used, greater understanding and acceptance of the concept might result. The term *flexible instructional organization* is proposed.[6]

SUMMARY

This chapter has been devoted to a discussion of differentiated staffing as it is being implemented in schools. Practice seems to indicate that a four-step hierarchy is becoming the dominant mode for categorizing the professional staff. The lowest-level or level-one teacher is usually a new teacher or an experienced teacher who desires limited responsibility. Level-two teachers are comparable to present classroom teachers. Level-three teachers are responsible for larger portions of the instructional program and perform coordinating functions in addition to some teaching responsibilities. Level-four teachers are at the top of the hierarchy and have the broadest range of responsibilities for large segments of the instructional program. A wide variety of paraprofessionals and aides are also utilized in the instructional program. Included in this group are instructional assistants, interns, clerical aides, and laymen who have specialized knowledge or skills.

[6] From this point on, the term *flexible instructional organization,* or *FIO,* will be used as a substitute for the terms *differentiated staffing* and *staffing differentiation.*

The move to differentiated staffing has had a profound effect on the organization and administration of schools. Decision making has been decentralized by authorizing that more decisions may be made at the building level. The instructional staff has also been brought into the decision-mak ing process at all levels. The total educative process has also been affected by staff differentiation. The curriculum has been revised to emphasize process and skill development and to provide for the present needs of students. Instruction is now characterized by flexible scheduling, individual instruction, flexible grouping, and more opportunities for students to pursue personal interests. To accommodate the revised curriculum and the variety of instructional methods, the school districts have altered their method of utilizing facilities. The change can be seen in the wide variety of ways in which space is used and, particularly, in the utilization of libraries and classrooms as learning centers. The centers are enriched environments which are used to extend classroom instruction, provide resources for independent study, motivate students, or provide remedial assistance.

Finally, as a result of the impact that differentiated staffing is having on the total school system, the position was taken that the terms *differentiated staffing* and *staff differentiation* are not appropriate to convey the principles and purposes of the concept. The primary purpose of differentiated staffing is to provide flexibility in the utilization of all resources to maximize the quality of education and to individualize instruction. Therefore, to avoid the confusion which surrounds the terms *differentiated staffing* and *staff differentiation,* the term *flexible instructional organization* was proposed as a substitute.

SELECTED BIBLIOGRAPHY

Arnold, Joseph P. "Applying Differentiated Staffing to Vocational-Technical Education." *Journal of Industrial Teacher Education, 7:* 13–20 (Fall 1969).

Association of Classroom Teachers. *Classroom Teachers Speak on Differentiated Teaching Assignments.* Report of the Classroom Teachers National Study Conference on Differentiated Teaching Assignments for Classroom Teachers. Washington, D.C.: The Association, a department of the National Education Association (1969), 32 pp.

English, Fenwick W. "Et Tu, Educator, Differentiated Staffing? Rationale and Model for a Differentiated Teaching Staff." *TEPS Write-in Papers on Flexible Staffing Patterns No. 4.* Washington, D.C.: National Commission on Teacher Education and Professional Standards, National Education Association (August 1969), 23 pp.

Florida State Department of Education, Division of Curriculum and Instruction. *Flexible Staff Organization Feasibility Study.* Interim Report. Tallahassee: The Department (February 1969), 40 pp.

Krumbein, Gerald. "How To Tell Exactly What Differentiated Staffing Will Cost Your District." *American School Board Journal, 157:* 19–24 (May 1970).

National School Public Relations Association. *Differentiated Staffing in the Schools: Education USA Special Report.* Washington, D.C.: The Association (1970), 48 pp.

Temple City, California

Introduction

Any thought of differentiated staffing almost instinctively brings to mind Temple City, California. It was here that the seed of an idea was planted, nourished, and grew into full bloom. The first exposure to differentiated staffing for most educators is to the Temple City model. Any recognition given to the developers of the model is justly deserved, for it is in Temple City that the viability of a new organization for instruction is demonstrated. The faculty and staff had little or no precedent to guide them as they attempted to make decisions during the planning of their model. School districts planning their own models now have a yardstick and guide to assist them. For these reasons, the Temple City model was selected for inclusion in this book.

The Temple City model has certain characteristics which appear to have been adopted by numerous other school districts. Major among these are professional self-regulation and collegial decision making. Professional self-regulation can be seen in the involvement of the professional staff in their own evaluation, selection of instructional leaders, and determining personnel policies and procedures. Collegial decision making is most evident in the instructional staff's representation on all decision-making bodies, including the school academic senate, the district academic senate, and the instructional council. The inclusion of instructional personnel in these groups is not "window dressing." The following statement of policy taken from the "Handbook of the Temple City Differentiated-Staffing Project" indicates the weight given to the opinions of the instructional staff.

> Where there is a difference of opinion which is considered significant by the principal or the majority of the Academic Senate, the following course of action should be taken within ten days in the stated order:
>
> 1. A request for an informal review session by the Superintendent and appropriate personnel should be made to explore possible solutions to the impasse.
> 2. If the informal review session does not resolve the impasse, it may be referred to the District Senate for review and decision. A brief must be developed which reflects the arguments of both sides and submitted to the Superintendent for distribution to the staff prior to the meeting. The Superintendent must call a meeting within ten school days after receiving the briefs to consider the problem.
>
> The school Academic Senate will name a party to represent each side before the District Senate. The principal is expected to make a report of his position on any issue under consideration. The District Senate may call in any other person as a resource in its deliberations. If a minority of the Academic Senate has appealed a decision, the District Senate has the privilege to review or refuse to hear a dispute. The Senate must give reasons for any declination on a referred problem.

3. If the District Senate and the Superintendent disagree over the decision reached in the Senate's deliberations, it may be appealed through the Superintendent for a final hearing before being submitted to the Board of Education. Such a presentation should be made as soon as possible.

As the oldest differentiated-staffing model, the Temple City model may well be the most fully developed model in the country. Attention should be called, particularly, to its well-developed definition of roles in its hierarchy and the well-defined policies and procedures for the selection and advancement of instructional staff members.

The Temple City model should prove to be an excellent source and guide for interested school districts.

TEMPLE CITY DIFFERENTIATED-STAFFING PROJECT

Michael Stover

The Temple City model of differentiated staffing is a massive and comprehensive change from the usual way in which American schools are organized. The model's components function more like the movement of a fine timepiece than jewels added to make a watch more durable. It can be hypothesized that differentiated staffing without the components of a comprehensive change model may or may not succeed; however, a comprehensive model is tantamount to a money-back guarantee. This is because the staffing innovation is carefully integrated with a new system for meeting educational needs. Instead of this innovation's being tacked onto an existing system, an entirely new system is designed and juxtaposed to the existing one. Changeover is started when the new system is matched with the existing one and is determined to be better. At this point, installation is initiated and changeover is completed.

The comprehensive model of staff differentiation has twelve components:

1. Differentiated roles and responsibilities
2. Flexible utilization of time and space (flexible scheduling)
3. Collegial evaluation processes
4. Diffusion of decision making
5. Curriculum vitalization
6. Teacher-dominated selection of teacher leaders
7. Utilization of teacher aides and clerks
8. Performance criteria for teacher evaluation
9. Specification of curricular objectives in performance or behavioral terms
10. Individualization of instruction
11. Installation of a multimedia support system
12. Initiation of a relevant and continuous program of in-service training

A school system organized to include these ingredients is designed so that the components are interfaced with a minimum of dysfunctions. Components can be individually justified but must be designed to support one another. What is created by the comprehensive model is a new organizational structure, not a jerry-built renovation of an existing structure. In the long run, it is far simpler to build a new structure than to patch up an old one. For example, commercial aircraft converted during World War II into combat warplanes were out-performed by specially designed aircraft with integrated components. Tacked-on combat components affected all areas of the converted aircraft's performance, making it an inferior weapon. Similarly, flexible scheduling added to a traditional school organization will, in all likelihood, fail because the staff is neither specialized nor organized to engage in curriculum renewal, teach in multiple instructional modes, or attempt master planning in terms of allocating time and space. Staff differentiation requires the time for professional activities outside of the classroom that is provided for by a flexible schedule. The Temple City model represents a new organizational structure that facilitates rather than neutralizes specific curricular and instructional innovations.

Comprehensive change can be justified by the failures of federally or privately funded projects in curricular and instructional innovations that are never successfully linked to the traditional school organization. Success might have been achieved if these innovations had been allowed to operate in a new organizational setting which encouraged curricular and instructional innovation.

DERIVATION OF THE TEMPLE CITY MODEL

The comprehensive Temple City model evolved from an initial staff concern that the reward system in education was not encouraging excellence. Moreover, the assumption that a teacher is a teacher was beginning to come in for some criticism. At this point in time, Dwight Allen, then of Stanford University, was invited during December of 1965 to address the Temple City Unified School District Administrative Workshop. What unfolded through Allen's presentation were the basic concepts of staff differentiation, especially the concept that there should be specialization of teacher talents. From this initial presentation, Allen worked with Temple City educators and presented a refinement of his ideas before a community workshop involving staff as well as PTA members and members of the board of education. Later, the superintendent of schools appointed a staff committee, headed by the principal of the district's junior high school, to draft a project for the Charles F. Kettering Foundation to fund a study in developing a differentiated teaching staff. Kettering accepted the proposed project and awarded the district $41,840. In the meantime, the superintendent of schools created the Differentiated Staffing Project Steering Committee to make the Kettering Fund study. After nine months of study, a key steering committee task force, the Teacher Job Analysis Task Force, developed a prototypic differentiated scheme of roles and responsibilities. The prototype was subsequently revised in the light of district resources and staff reaction.

The Planning Process

The basis of this comprehensive change is a problem-solving model which utilizes the needs of staff, students, and society as its starting point. These are the clients whose needs must be satisfied by the school system. Their needs were determined by data collected by in-district and out-of-district personnel. From an analysis of these needs, an educational system was structured with provisions for change from time to time as new needs evolve. Figure 1 depicts this problem-solving model. Hard data concerning learner needs came from an in-district report of graduates of Temple City High School, which was prepared by Temple City teachers and administrators organized for this purpose as a differentiated-staffing steering committee. The pioneering work in determining teacher needs was done by the Arthur D. Little Company. Educational Testing Service made an important contribution by determining the needs of society.[1]

This data was processed by members of the steering committee who formed the membership of various committees

[1] Learner needs are measured by the *Temple City High School Five Year Follow-Up Study*, 1963. Teacher needs are reflected in the *Report on Teacher Supply and Demand, 1965–1975;* for the California State Board of Education by the Arthur D. Little Company and in *Supply and Demand in Public Schools, 1967,* published by the National Education Association. Societal needs are measured by *A Plan for Evaluating the Educational Programs in Pennsylvania.* It is expected that revisions will be made as the staffing model is implemented. This will provide constant analysis of the relative adequacy and validity of the goals, operational definitions, and criteria for the goals of differentiated staffing.

FIGURE 1
Project Mission Profile

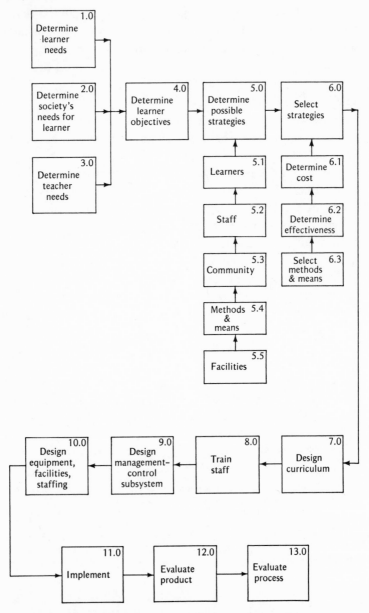

and special task forces to study the implications of alternative staffing patterns. Some patterns had legal implications. California law, for instance, requires that 55 percent of school district budgets be spent on teacher salaries; however, the employment of needed clerks and teacher assistants as envisioned in most differentiated staffs might make the overall figure for Temple City schools dip below that level. Other staffing plans had financial implications that created problems. One comprehensive model had to be overhauled when it was found to be beyond the capacity of local resources.

In evaluating the various staffing patterns, the steering committee members looked for certain basic characteristics:

1. The new staffing pattern had to be supportable by the school district's current tax base and not be dependent upon external financial assistance beyond the initial installation period.
2. The new staffing model had to create an alternative system of rewards to that of school administration so that classroom teaching would have career incentives for teachers.
3. The new staffing model had to provide the essence of a profession of teaching, for example, professional self-regulation, teacher-dominated selection of teacher leaders, and collegial decision making.
4. The new staffing model had to provide for a systematic means of linking the school system with the latest research being conducted by national projects and colleges and universities.

Creation of the steering committee reflected the concern of educators over the professional status of today's teacher in the decision-making process of education. Although the average California teacher has more than five years of college training, he is most often not involved in the decisions made for his area of expertise. The steering committee was organized to manage the school system's study of differentiated staffing and had elected representation from all schools, plus ex officio membership of local NEA and AFT representatives.

THE TEMPLE CITY MODEL

The differentiated-staffing model currently in use in Temple City may be described in a variety of ways. One frequently used typology involves the degree of *vertical* or *horizontal differentiation*. Vertical differentiation is a staffing plan patterned according to specialized responsibilities in addition to classroom teaching, such as curriculum development, research, and in-service teacher education. Horizontal differentiation occurs when responsibilities are classified along lines such as teacher and clerk, small-group instructor and large-group lecturer, English teacher and mathematics teacher. The Temple City model differentiates somewhat horizontally in that it recognizes a hierarchy of tasks, some of which are performed exclusively by clerks while others are provided for by teachers. Subject-area specialization or departmentalization is also part of the Temple City model. The model, however, is primarily a vertical differentiation of roles.

The vertical differentiation used in Temple City has the responsibility of classroom teaching interwoven into each classification. Beyond this, the roles vary greatly in responsibilities and compensation. The Temple City model is a four-level differentiation of roles. Table 1 depicts its major features. Salaries range from $7,539 to $22,065, depending on role and responsibility. The roles can also be compared and contrasted in terms of months in annual contract, tenure, status in the decision-making system, percentage of time spent in the classroom, method of selection, means of evaluation, and total number of positions in each classification.

To simplify matters it is possible to assign at this point a

TABLE 1
Career Ladder

Tenure	Tenure	Nontenure	Nontenure
			Master teacher Doctorate or equivalent
		Senior teacher M.A. or equivalent	
	Staff teacher B.A.		
Associate teacher B.A.			
100% teaching responsibility	100% teaching responsibility	2/3 Staff teaching responsibility	1/3 Staff teaching responsibility
10 months $7,539–$9,977 73 positions	10 months $7,539–$14,590 74 positions	11 months $14,157–$17,716 25 positions	11 months $17,500–$22,065 3 positions
Resource-center aide		$3,078–$3,740	
Clerks $4,560–$5,540			

descriptive word or two for each role. The associate-teacher role can be described as "the beginner." The phrase "old pro" best depicts the staff-teacher role. The senior teacher position is that of curriculum and in-service man, while research and development characterize the master-teacher role.

Flexible Scheduling

To clearly conceive the responsibility range of the various teaching positions it is necessary to jump ahead a little and

bring in one of the components of a comprehensive model of differentiated staffing—the flexible utilization of time and space. This is the concept of flexible scheduling in which the school day is broken into time periods of varying lengths. This allows some classes to meet longer than others. Also, it allows students to be grouped into large and small classes or be unscheduled as to grouping and thereby freed to work in independent study centers. Time allowed for independent study may range from 25 to 50 percent of the school day. The Stanford School Scheduling System employed by Temple City Schools provides for 40 percent of the school day to be unscheduled for the average secondary student. The figure is slightly less for an upper-elementary student. This flexibility of time and space differs strikingly from the self-contained classroom of 30 students, 30-by-30-foot construction, with 1-hour time periods.

The Associate Teacher

In self-contained classrooms the differences in assignments and responsibilities between associate and staff teachers would be difficult to ascertain and are not as visible. Since the Temple City model is based on scheduling flexibility, it provides opportunities for pupils and neophyte teachers to be grouped in configurations which match the task level of the associate teacher role with the instructional needs of a homogeneous group of students. The associate teachers' assignments do not require them to meet the needs of a broad diversity of student abilities.

The associate teacher is most often a neophyte to the teaching profession. He is expected to quickly attain specialist status in one of the three instructional modes of large and small group or tutorial (independent) study. He is in the process of developing subject-matter expertise and gaining experience with a variety of curricular formats; thus, he is responsible for the application of a curriculum unit, but is not expected to be able to design complete units. He does, however, have a formal role in curriculum evaluation. His teaching load includes tutorial time as a regular assignment, but as a member of a disciplinary or cross-disciplinary teaching team he is expected to contribute to the total welfare of all children within the scope of his team.

Besides the beginning teacher, there is a second type of teacher that may be an associate teacher. This person may be characterized as one who views his employment as something less than a career. Consequently, he is not motivated to pursue a program of professional growth. A female teacher with family responsibilities might fall into this category. The designers of the Temple City model believe that there should be a place in education for these persons.

The Staff Teacher

The staff teacher, the "old pro," is experienced and a specialist in at least two modes of instruction. His responsibilities reflect his greater experience as a professional. Staff-teacher assignments include a broader range of pupil diversity. Staff teachers form a cadre of experienced teachers who do not desire responsibilities outside the classroom. As in the case of the associate teacher, differentiation is much more difficult if the school structure does not provide much room for teacher specialization and utilization to occur beyond traditional "class swapping" of teachers over time.

The staff teacher has definite curriculum-development responsibilities. He is expected to prepare and apply teacher-prepared curricula for a broad student base, and his curricular units are evaluated for appropriateness by his colleagues. As contrasted to the associate teacher, the staff teacher shapes the total instructional program more deeply via participation in the development of curriculum and the professional evaluation process. He makes important evaluative decisions affecting the employment of his teaching-team leader, the senior teacher.

The Senior Teacher

The senior-teacher position represents the first major break with tradition in terms of functions and responsibilities above the staff level. It is often averred that only teaching ability should be the basis for differentiation above the staff level. If this were the case, we would not have differentiation of tasks, but merit pay in disguise. Some teachers would earn more because they were perceived to be better teachers by certain criteria. It would be very difficult to show how differentiation would occur by attempting to describe such differences in teachers without resorting to vague and highly subjective procedures consistently rejected by teachers themselves. Merit pay compensates teachers who are better; differentiated staffing pay teachers who have added responsibilities.

Teaching may be conceived as a business requiring not only a treatment or an application, but also a diagnosis or an evaluation as well. Teacher planning time is certainly not an administratively oriented job if it includes pupil diagnosis, selection and evaluation of teaching strategies for learners, or methods of application and evaluation. The time the teacher is actually with children, that is, the client, constitutes only one part of a teacher's responsibilities. As in other professions, this is a responsibility which is easiest to delegate. In medicine, for example, the physician spends his time in diagnosis; the patient may be treated by a nurse or other medical aide, or may treat himself. This has also been the case with the employment of clerks or teacher assistants. Once the teacher has diagnosed and prescribed, a paraprofessional may supply the treatment or it may be supplied by a teaching team.

Aspects of the "educational treatment" that probably cannot be delegated are those skills in assisting pupils to think or to solve problems; these require the assistance of a highly trained adult to motivate, assist, and evaluate. The teacher is an impartial judge of pupil effort or a sympathetic and warm adult stimulating the acquisition of new skills.

Differentiation of tasks may therefore be spread out to other aspects of what teachers do, which may be more highly specialized, and which affect significantly what all pupils may learn. This forms the basis for the creation of the senior- and master-teacher roles. Their responsibilities and "differentiated" functions extend into curriculum development, colleague evaluation, instructional specialization, and increased coordination and responsibility for what students collectively learn in their areas of expertise. In addition, the Temple City model recognizes the need for the involvment of instructional personnnel in the administrative decision-making machinery.

Senior teachers are primarily responsible for the application of curricular and instructional innovations to the classroom. Their role may be described as putting educational innovations into effect in the classroom and subjecting them to the modifications which arise from day-to-day experience. Out of this work should emerge refined curriculum, sound in theory and practical in the light of classroom experience.

Senior teachers are the master practitioners in their area. They are exemplary teachers who possess a great deal of experience and training and who have remained vital and imaginative. They conduct in-service classes, workshops, and seminars for teachers in exemplary techniques and methods in subject or skill areas.

Other important responsibilities include:

1. Assignment and effective utilization of student teachers and educational assistants

2. Planning with the teaching team the school schedule and pupil programming
3. Development of pilot programs for implementing new curricula
4. Refinement of methods to work with individuals, subject matter, and skills

In addition, senior teachers are responsible for a variety of tasks clustered as fiscal management, communications, decision making, human relations, and personnel evaluation. Because of the nature of some of these clusters, some critics have maintained that senior teachers may become quasi-administrators in a model of staff differentiation. This is possible, but the responsibility for determining whether the senior teacher shuffles papers or actually performs needed services rests with the teachers who design his job. If they emphasize the administrative, the senior teacher will be an administrator. The successful functioning of a senior teacher is as much dependent upon the integrity of the staff and associate teachers as it is upon the senior teacher himself.

Senior teachers perform additional functions according to their disciplinary or cross-disciplinary area. A stipulation of all the tasks senior teachers might attempt is beyond the range of this report, because school staffs develop particular job descriptions each year. If the senior teacher has successfully fulfilled the needs of his teachers, their needs will have changed; therefore, it is necessary to rewrite the job descriptions each year.

Senior teachers also serve as chairmen of school teaching teams. Their teams may be composed of teachers in their curricular area or may be from different curricular areas in a cross-disciplinary team. The former means of organization is most common and is the preferred pattern at the secondary level. Experimental attempts are being made in Temple City at the elementary level with the cross-disciplinary teaming of teachers.

The Master Teacher

The master teacher is considered the school system's "self-renewal" agent, bringing to the system the latest thought in his curricular area. It is this person who has the primary responsibility for maintaining the vitality and relevance of subject-matter content, form, and related teaching strategies. The master teacher possesses a scholarly depth of knowledge in subject matter or skills areas that enables him to evaluate critically emerging research, and from it select those ideas, practices, and principles that will contribute to the development of new instructional methods and programs. He retrieves and translates research into experimental instructional probes with his senior-teacher colleagues. He formulates, with the senior teachers in his curricular area, master plans for his subject area, which include the designing of the school program and schedules, and utilization of new courses.

While senior teachers are school based, master teachers have district-wide responsibilities. In Temple City this means kindergarten through senior high school. Together, senior and master teachers constitute vertical curriculum committees charged with scope and sequence for their subject area.

In some ways, the title master teacher is misleading. The master teacher is not the master teacher because he stands on a pinnacle of teaching excellence. This would mean that merit pay has been installed. The role is so named because in the Temple City model it has the broadest range of responsibilities which are directly rooted in classroom teaching.

Among his functions are:

1. Directing with colleagues in-service classes, workshops, discussion groups, and preparation of faculty monographs
2. Writing projects for funding probes

3. Designing new curricula in harmony with the best available curriculum theory and design
4. Formulating with staff subject-area master plans and working with senior and staff teachers in designing the school program, schedule, utilization of resources, educational objectives, and organization of new courses
5. Establishing and maintaining a continual program of research and evaluation
6. Translating related research into experimental instructional probes with senior teacher colleagues

Particular indexes of task accomplishment developed for the master teacher of social science include his research responsibilities to:

1. Disseminate orally and in writing to the senior teachers and staff, reports and information on research and innovation in social studies curriculum development, new materials, and processes
2. Identify useful instructional materials, books, programs, curricula, research studies and summaries, and the like, useful for demonstrating the theory and practice of new social studies and in-service programs
3. Develop research and experimental design for the empirical validation of new materials, teaching strategies, and exemplary social studies programs

Instructional Aides

Horizontal differentiation in the Temple City model is evidenced by the creation of a number of clerk and teacher-assistant positions. Under flexible scheduling, assistants are necessary for the supervision and management of independent study facilities. Skills involved include ability to relate effectively with students and adults and to assume responsibility for their behavior during supervised study; knowledge of modern office methods and practices; ability to type and file rapidly and accurately; knowledge of common library procedures and techniques; ability to work cooperatively with others; interest in subject matter; and ability to help create a learning atmosphere in which students will want to learn.

The Job Analysis Committee of the differentiated staffing steering committee determined that under the then-existing staffing and organizational plan, 22 percent of the school day was devoted by teachers to clerical matters. The committee recommended that the differentiated teacher spend approximately 4 percent of his time on clerical matters. This change in emphasis is facilitated by the employment of clerks and teacher assistants.

DIFFERENTIATED COMPENSATION

As previously suggested, the differentiated roles of the Temple City model may also be described in terms of a number of factors other than responsibilities. In terms of salaries, each succeeding position on the differentiated staff pays more and is based on a "whole-job" concept whereby separate salary schedules are established for each role.

The beginning salary for the associate-teacher level is approximately equivalent to starting salaries of other school systems in the surrounding area which compete for beginning teachers. The beginning and maximum steps for senior teachers are comparable to those of a building principal with an equivalent working year because of the comparability in qualifications and responsibilities. Similarly, the beginning and maximum steps for a master teacher are comparable to those for a 12-month administrator with district-wide responsibilities, for example, an assistant superintendent. Salary ranges for each role are indicated in Table 2. Initial placement on the associate-teacher and standard-teacher salary

TABLE 2

Temple City Model Differentiated Salary Schedules, 1970–1971

Associate-Teacher		
Step	(year)	Annual salary
1		$7,539
2		$7,857
3		$8,175
4		$8,493
5		$8,811
6		$9,129
7		$9,449
8		$9,977

Standard-Teacher[a]		
Step	Class	Annual salary
1	I	$ 7,539
5	II	$ 8,853
7	III	$10,123
9	IV	$11,606
11	V	$14,590

[a]Staff teachers are paid on this schedule. A new schedule embracing the principles of the other differentiated schedules is in the process of preparation.

Senior-Teacher		
Step	(year)	Annual salary
1		$14,157
2		$15,055
3		$15,943
4		$16,831
5		$17,716

Master-Teacher		
Step	(year)	Annual salary
1		$17,500
2		$18,641
3		$19,782
4		$20,023
5		$22,065

schedules credits a combination of out-of-state and California experience not to exceed five years. The following placement criteria is applicable to the senior- and master-teacher salary schedules:

1. In order to compensate for the additional time and responsibility factors, placement on the senior-teacher salary

schedule shall be on the step which is closest to, but not less than $2500 over previous placement on the standard-teacher salary schedule.

2. Placement on the master-teacher salary schedule shall be negotiated by the assistant superintendent for personnel, in consideration of previous responsibility, salary, work year, and the recommendation of the selection committee.

3. Extra assignments during the working day for senior teachers, such as coaching, newspaper editing, performing arts assignments, and summer school teaching, shall be approved by the staff served by the senior teacher, the school senate, the steering committee, and the district senate.

4. There shall be no extra compensation for any assignment conducted during the regular working day. Consultant fees for work outside the district must be earned only on days charged against accrued vacation.

TENURE AND EVALUATION

Tenure is earned after three successful years as an associate or staff teacher. It is granted for senior and master teachers as staff teachers only. Tenure is not granted to persons holding the advanced positions, because of the principle of service. The designers of the Temple City model made the jobs of senior and master teachers subject to the felt needs of the recipients who were to be "served" by those positions. Long experience with the authoritarian supervisor had convinced teachers that they wanted no more of having things foisted upon them in the guise of service. In order to avoid having the senior teacher end up as a supervisor with part-time class-room teaching responsibilities, the model's designers built into the concept a nontenure status. Other principles include the following:

1. Teaching colleagues were to select their teaching leaders.

2. Teaching colleagues would have a majority on selection panels.
3. Teaching colleagues were to design the job to be performed by those in the advanced roles.
4. Teachers receiving the services of those in the advanced positions were to evaluate the effectiveness of such services.

Evaluation is based on a dual system that is collegial and reciprocal. Under differentiated staffing, the advanced roles are regarded as service and leadership functions. Measuring the quality of these functions required that teachers receiving the services of or being guided by the individual in the advanced role be part of the personnel evaluative process. Thus, the reason for two-way evaluation: Those receiving the services are in the best position to ascertain the relevance of the services. Moreover, teacher-specialists holding the advanced positions are in the best position, because of their training and day-to-day contact, to measure the contribution made by team members. Performance is measured according to specific indexes of task accomplishment developed for each position at the time of employment.

ADVANCEMENT POLICIES AND PROCEDURES

Teachers are not selected for advancement on the basis of someone's judgment about their performance. Rather, as openings become available, teaching personnel are given the option of applying for the positions and being selected by a panel of colleagues who will be working with them at their respective assignments. The number of such colleagues serving on the selection panels for associate and staff teachers is left to each school to determine. Selection committees for senior teachers are composed of two teachers elected by the teaching staff within the discipline or area being considered, from the school in which the proposed senior teacher is to function; an outside university specialist in the discipline; the principal of the school; and the assistant superintendent for personnel. For the master teacher, the selection panel adds one teacher and requires that each of the three be elected from each respective level of the system organization, that is, primary, upper-elementary, and secondary. The panel also includes the superintendent of schools, as well as the assistant superintendent for personnel. The school principals are represented by one principal, whom they choose. An outside university specialist is included, as is the case with the senior-teacher selection panel.

The length of contract for the advanced roles is 11 months. The added month provides time for curriculum development through subject-area vertical curriculum committees.

There are no academic requirements other than a valid teaching credential for the four levels of teachers. Experience, however, indicates that selection committees consider a master's degree as a benchmark for academic qualifications for a senior-teacher position and a doctorate for the master-teacher role.

All teachers teach, although the time they spend in the classroom varies from classification to classification. Associate and staff teachers are in classroom situations 50 to 60 percent of the time under a flexible schedule allowing 40 percent unscheduled time for independent study by students. Senior teachers are in the classroom one-third to one-half of the school day. Master teachers do varying degrees of demonstration teaching of new techniques or curricular content, teaching approximately one-quarter to one-third of the day.

COSTING-OUT MODEL

The number of teachers in each job classification is directly related to available district resources. Wealthy school systems are able to deploy additional advanced roles over moderate income systems, such as that of Temple City. Temple City schools, employing a 175-member teaching staff to service 4600 youngsters, has decided on this ratio in each classification:

Associate teachers	73 positions	(42 percent)
Staff teachers	74 positions	(42 percent)
Senior teachers	25 positions	(14 percent)
Master teachers	3 positions	(2 percent)

Based on the premise that the new staffing pattern would not be more costly than the traditional pattern, provisions were built into the Temple City model that limit the number of holders of each position. Since the previous average teacher salary was well above that of the typical associate teacher, an increase in the number of the associate teacher positions provides funds for additional advanced roles. The district's capacity to pay the excess costs of a minimum of 25 senior teachers was reinforced by a recent cost study conducted by the district's personnel office. The study is grounded on the assumption that the advanced roles are funded by savings generated by employing teachers on the associate-teacher salary schedule. Studies of the actual cost of the teaching staff before differentiated staffing and each year since provide a reliable formula for projecting the minimum-savings differential each time an associate teacher is added to the staff. This saving currently averages $666, or approximately 40 percent of the difference between the average departing teacher's salary and that of the replacement. Based upon the anticipated rate of increase in associate teachers, the district will reach a desired ratio of 50 percent of staff on the associate-teacher salary schedule by 1979–1980. When that occurs, the distribution of staff on the various salary schedules will be similar to that of the staff in 1964–1965, when half of the staff was on the first two classifications of the district's standard salary schedule. Additional advanced roles will be deployed over time as savings offset excess costs of the roles. The district during 1970–1971 had a total of a master teacher and 24 senior teachers, including interns and trainees who are paid lump-sum stipends instead of being placed on the senior-teacher salary schedule.

Full deployment of the Temple City model will take years, because a provision was written into the differentiated-staffing project stating that no teacher would earn less under a differentiated staff than he earned when it was first instituted. This "grandfather clause" protects staff employed prior to the district's entry into differentiated staffing; the provision does not apply, however, to newly hired staff. Therefore, the exact date of completion of the staffing model is dependent on staff attrition. Although this process is time-consuming, it has the value of providing security to significant segments of the staff whose support is vital to the success of this educational innovation.

DECISION MAKING

The differentiated roles also vary in terms of participation in the decision-making process. Associate and staff teachers participate through their teaching teams, the basic units of school district organization under the Temple City model. The teams establish work priorities, coordinate the specialties of teachers in curricular topics, prepare and administer team budgets, operate learning centers, prepare time and space requirements for master scheduling, develop and implement curriculum, and supervise aides and student teachers. The chairman of each team, the senior teacher, is a member of the school academic senate and the vertical curriculum committee in his curricular area. The school senate is responsible for the educational program of the school. This responsibility and its corresponding authority for decision making is as broad as instructional problems demand. Typical functions include coordination of personnel employment, evaluation, and discipline, preparation and administration of the school budget, and interdepartmental relations. School senates are composed of senior teachers and the school principal, who serves as chairman with power of appeal to the district senate but without an administrative veto over senate decisions. Senior teachers, along with their master teacher, constitute vertical curriculum committees that are responsible for curricular scope and sequence.

Senior teachers may also serve as their school representative to the district senate, the overall policy-making body of the school system composed of principals and two teachers from each school. The superintendent of schools acts as chairman. This body resolves disputes among individual school academic senates and recommends to the board of education the district budget and other important policies.

Master teachers are chairmen of the vertical curriculum committees, but are not members of school or district senates. Their expertise gains them membership on the district instructional council, which is responsible for developing an integrated district curriculum that achieves educational goals approved by the board of education. The instructional council is a recommending body to the district senate.

The Temple City model does not provide for democracy in decision making; it does provide a representative technocracy, that is, decision making by those who are expert in the type of decision being made.

CURRICULUM VITALIZATION

Curriculum is vitalized when teachers can apply the latest research to student and societal needs in a form that students can master through various learning modes, under the guidance of a professional, in a work environment conducive to creativity. The comprehensive model of differentiated staffing provides this through differentiating roles and responsibilities, flexibility in utilizing time and space, evaluating of personnel by fellow colleagues, and diffusing decision making. The pioneering work of McGregor, Gellerman, and Likert in organizational climate, productivity, and creativity underscores the need for a healthy work environment. This is facilitated whenever teachers are treated as professionals and given the major voice in establishing organizational objectives through a diffusion of decision-making authority.

IMPLEMENTING THE TEMPLE CITY MODEL

Oak Avenue Intermediate School, the district's lone junior high, was selected as the pilot school. It was remodeled so as to accommodate flexible scheduling, knocking down walls to convert traditional 30-by-30-foot classroom boxes into small- and large-group rooms and subject-matter resource centers. A complement of three senior teachers in the major subject areas were hired for Oak Avenue. Transition procedures were initiated at the district level to convert the 175-member nondifferentiated staff to the four-level teacher differentiation. A training program funded by the U.S. Office of Education involved 40 staff members who sought to become senior or master teachers. Eighteen months later, the district deployed an additional 21 senior-teacher positions at its five other schools. Elementary flexible scheduling was tried successfully at two schools for grades 3 through 6. The district's primary school piloted a cross-disciplinary differentiation whereby a team of teachers headed by a senior teacher is responsible for the continuous-progress education of 150 students. From the model's initial implementation at Oak Avenue Intermediate School, it grew until it now fully encompasses the school system from grades kindergarten to 12.

IN-SERVICE EDUCATION

The U.S. Office of Education through the Education Professions Development Act demonstrated its interest in the staffing innovation by funding projects at 28 sites across the nation in 1970–1971. Federal participation in Temple City was first limited to senior- and master-teacher candidates and trainees, but was later extended to all staff members of the district from associate teachers to school administrators. Now, training is divided into two major phases, leadership training and monthly total-staff workshops. The leadership training is conducted through biweekly sessions involving 43 district leaders in areas such as organizational analysis, group dynamics, model building, survey of innovations, and instructional-management studies. Total-staff training is accomplished through monthly special-interest workshops and followed up with individualized training by senior teachers. Workshops are conducted in such areas as video-tape recording, the inquiry method for small-group instruction, the audio-tutorial method, and the remedial student. Thirteen workshops are offered each month for staff selection.

A continuous in-service training program is the twelfth element of the comprehensive model. It flourishes in a school system which is not hindered by traditional organizational ills such as rigid scheduling, pyramidal power and stereotyped roles. Although in-service programs are typically created to meet staff needs and impart skills, these skills may often be useless in the traditional organization. This is because their actual need may have arisen as a result of existing organizational ills. In-service education under the comprehensive model encourages staff members to develop a repertoire of skills that can be used in the creative environment fostered by flexible use of time and space, individualized instruction, and differentiated roles and responsibilities.

The training program is perpetual under the comprehensive model. Senior and master teachers and school administrators are trained, and they, in turn, train the total staff. The latest instructional techniques and content are broadly communicated within the school system and are developed into training sessions taught by senior and master teachers. The training program, beyond an initial installation period, is self-supporting and is not dependent upon external inputs. Consultants need not be hired, since the system employs a number of in-house scholars as master teachers. Although the staff may be encouraged to attend university and college classes, many staff needs will be satisfied by in-service education.

EVALUATION OF THE TEMPLE CITY MODEL

Evaluations conducted to date of the local model have made the following findings:

1. Educational costs have remained stable.
2. Student achievement scores are better or no worse than before.
3. Teachers have more time to plan.
4. Students express an overwhelmingly favorable attitude toward flexible scheduling.
5. Staff members overwhelmingly support differentiated staffing as a means to improve learning.
6. Community members support the concept 2 to 1, although

some have reservations about aspects of flexible scheduling.

7. Utilization of multimedia resources are many times greater at schools with the comprehensive model than at similarly situated schools.

8. The advanced roles are overwhelmingly valued by staff.

Evaluation of the program is an ongoing process involving in-house personnel under the leadership of the district's evaluation committee, chaired by the district psychologist, as well as external agencies such as the U.S. Office of Education and the California State Department of Education. In addition, a number of school districts have sent survey teams to the district and have published evaluative reports. Survey instruments have ranged from locally prepared attitude questionnaires to cost analysis by the state department of education, to in-depth interviews with affected members by project and external personnel.

CONTINUING PROBLEMS

Trade-off paraprofessional costs, further individualization of instruction, further development of teacher skills in the higher levels of learning identified by Bloom, Krathwold *et al.,* and improved articulation of the primary through secondary curriculum are major challenges that face Temple City educators. The comprehensive model encourages a variety of approaches to meeting these challenges. For example, the advanced roles have as part of their job descriptions the investigation and utilization of alternative means of individualized instruction. Improved articulation is the task of the vertical curriculum committees which up to this time have focused on reaching agreement on terminal objectives for the primary, upper-elementary, junior high school, and high school levels. Further work is being done in specifying the entire range of skills vital for graduates of the system. Beyond this, a broad elective program is being developed.

CONCLUSION

In designing differentiated-staffing models, educators would do well to keep three principles in mind:

1. Know your objectives.
2. Know your staff and community.
3. Know your resources.

From these principles, a comprehensive model can be developed that reflects local needs. The Temple City model is a portrait of Temple City objectives, resources, staff and community. In this sense it is unique. The Temple City model, on the other hand, also demonstrates how a school system can innovate comprehensive change. This process is replicable and should be worth close study.

There are limitations, and Fenwick English, director of differentiated staffing from 1966 until 1970, had some in mind when he wrote finis to Temple City Schools and went on to pursue new challenges:

> Five years have seen a lot of water under the bridge in Temple City. We have seen unprecedented change, confusion, and accomplishment. . . . It was here that differentiated staffing became a reality; it was proven to be something which by the very fact it happened was not within the realm of human responses as a concrete alternative; it wasn't and isn't the Boeing 707, and like the Wright Brothers' first 200+ airborne feet, spectacular only in the sense it has never been done before. . . . Differentiated staffing is a structural innovation. It aims to change aspects of the school structure that inhibit a viable teacher response to students. As such, however, it does not guarantee that the response will happen, it simply encourages and rewards that response when given. Only the teacher can make it happen. . . .

Sarasota County, Florida

Introduction

The Sarasota County model was originally selected for inclusion for two reasons. First, as a county school district, it had to overcome the handicap of introducing an innovation in a school district which spans many miles. Second, it is a relatively large school district in terms of population. The author saw a need for including a relatively large school district to illustrate that size is not necessarily a handicap to developing a flexible instructional organization. This proved to be a most fortuitous choice. It was possible to include not only a relatively large school district, but also some innovative solutions to problems faced by almost any school district in the process of developing an FIO model.

First, a method was devised for the allocation of resources which permits each school in the district to determine a staffing pattern to meet its particular needs. Second, a relatively simple method for allowing greater flexibility in the utilization of time during the school day was developed. While it may not provide the flexibility possible when a computer is used for this purpose, most schools do not have computer capabilities. Consequently, Sarasota County's solution should prove useful for the majority of school districts. Third, the concept of adjunct teacher is introduced. School districts have been prevented by certification laws from utilizing the unique knowledges and skills of laymen in the instructional program. The policies and procedures established by Sarasota County for the utilization of specially skilled laymen appears to have overcome all previous restrictions.

In any discussion of flexible instructional organization, the question usually asked is "What will it cost?" Whatever response was given, it was usually based on conjecture. In the report of the Sarasota model which follows, a comparison is shown between traditional and differentiated staffing patterns. The significance of the comparison is not in the fact that the cost was almost the same for each pattern, but rather in the increase in benefits derived from the differentiated pattern. For an increase of approximately 1 percent in expenditures, Venice Junior High School was able to increase the number of electives available to its students and reduce the adult-to-student ratio from approximately 20 to 1 to 15 to 1. Therefore, the increase can easily be justified on the basis of return for dollar invested.

A few words here about the Venice Junior High School building may assist the reader in placing the implementation of the Sarasota County model in a realistic perspective. Completed in 1958, the Venice Junior High School was designed to accommodate 579 students. The present enrollment is 834 students. The bright and airy appearance of this 1-story building was from the beginning somewhat idealistic even for Florida's ideal climate. Students who must walk across the campus for lunch at the high school cafeteria or spend their physical education periods out-of-doors can and do get wet and cold. There is no area where students can eat lunch or congregate during lunch time.

In addition to 20 standard classrooms, the original building also has a unit housing a band room, chorus room, and a locker and shower facility which is used by both boys and girls to dress for physical education. Art and shop courses are assigned to standard-sized classrooms that are inadequate for such activities. A small 2-story unit contains administrative offices, clinic, and a teachers' lounge on the first floor and a library on the second. In 1964, a 6-room science wing was added and an adequate library was built in 1969. This freed the second floor of the administrative unit for a suite of offices and lounge. One by one, eight portable classrooms have been trailed in to huddle dismally on the periphery of the building. Aesthetically, the school is satisfactory. The architecture is charming, if impractical, but the lack of a gymnasium, lunchroom, and auditorium—basic needs of any school—coupled with overcrowding, add up to a definitely substandard facility for any type of program.

The fact that the Venice Junior High School has been able to implement an FIO model in the quarters available to it seems to indicate that physical facilities are not a limiting factor in a flexible instructional organization.

A SYSTEM MODEL OF DIFFERENTIATED STAFFING: THE SCHOOL BOARD OF SARASOTA COUNTY, FLORIDA

Gene M. Pillot

The needs which cause educators to examine promising new approaches to instruction may range from solving serious problems in some districts to fine-tuning of smoothly functioning programs in more fortunate school systems. Differentiated staffing is an innovation with potential application at both extremes. Its promise of a career ladder for teachers, shared decision making by those most knowledgeable in each area of instruction, and the maximizing of individualization of instruction through flexible and efficient use of human, material, and time resources are the attributes that make the concept of differentiated staffing attractive to a school system at any position on a continuum of quality. Sarasota County, Florida in May, 1968 was no exception. The Board of Public Instruction, administration, staff, and teachers' association were united in a desire to provide the best possible education for the youth of the community. They saw the principles of differentiated staffing as a means to maximize the quality and results of the educational program for the dollar spent.

Staff involvement in the study, planning, design, and implementation of staff differentiation is *the* major criterion for potential success. The literature on differentiated staffing includes a number of examples of concern, hesitation, suspicion, and rejection of the innovation by teachers where insufficient or no involvement of staff was provided. In Sarasota, the commitment was made early that differentiated staffing would not be imposed. Teachers, with support of the board and central administration, were given the opportunity to study, evaluate, and decide its potential value to the school system. The Sarasota County Teachers' Association (SCTA), central administration, and interested staff of several schools joined in a 2-year study that led to the design and implementation of the model described in this report. The Board of Public Instruction authorized the formation of a Central Steering Committee on Differentiated Staffing, and recognized it as the advisory council on all related matters. This committee included representatives of all divisions of staff, instructional and noninstructional, and the SCTA. Each of the 24 members was elected by the group he represented to serve a 2-year term. The committee membership consisted of 12 classroom teachers, 3 supervisors, 4 administrators, 1 business-services representative, 2 lay citizens, 1 SCTA representative, and a board member (ex officio). All models, salary schedules, implementation procedures, and other decisions regarding differentiated staffing were submitted to and endorsed by the steering committee before presentation to the school board.

All schools had been invited to participate in the study and implementation at any time. None had been directed or persuaded to do so. Of 26 schools, 8 participated in the study and 4 implemented the model fully or partially in September 1970.

The study in Sarasota resulted in an early determination that any model designed should provide to each school an opportunity to design its staffing pattern according to its unique goals, needs, and philosophy; while at the same time conforming to certain minimum school-system standards of staff allocation, job specifications, salaries, and instructional program. The outcome of the study[1] was a model called a *system model,* so named for its application to an entire school system.

The system model is a conceptual plan by which a school system provides its component schools the means for implementing a staff-differentiation model designed by the individual school according to its unique instructional environment. This quality is called autonomy.

The school is able to adapt its individual model to any substantial change that may occur in the instructional environment by selecting a different staffing pattern from the school-system model. That quality is called fluidity.

Most school systems develop personal criteria for staff allocation, job specifications, and salaries that are applied equitably within the district. In a given school system, each school staffed under the provisions of the system model would be allocated staff units by the same formula and would use those units to select its staff from the vertical hierarchy of the staffing submodel. Each job classification of the vertical hierarchy would have similar job specifications in schools of like size and grade-level organization. Finally, each staff member in a particular job classification of the vertical hierarchy would be paid on the same salary schedule. These

[1] Gene Pillot, "Conceptual Design of a System Model of Differentiated Staffing," D.Ed. diss., University of Florida, 1970.

procedures of allocation, selection, job requirements, and remuneration provide minimum consistency in the organization of every school staff with the school-system personnel policies.

Differentiated staffing may be defined simply as an efficient utilization of resources to maximize the quality and individualization of instruction. Whether stated as broad goals, as specific objectives for positive change in learner behavior, or in a form somewhere between those extremes, most schools or school districts will have a set of guidelines for the curriculum and instructional program. The system model is designed to provide sufficient flexibility and possible staffing combinations to permit a school to organize its staff in the pattern considered best suited for conducting the instructional program of the school. This quality is called extensibility —the capability of the system model concept or components to be adapted to other school systems.

These four qualities—autonomy, fluidity, minimum consistency, and extensibility—are realized by the selection of an individual school model from the staffing submodel, and the implementation of that school model according to the elements of the implementation submodel.

THE STAFFING SUBMODEL

The staffing submodel is designed to organize the instructional staff into a logical vertical and horizontal differentiation that is based upon the totality of tasks performed in the school program, a classification of those tasks into major subdivisions of the program, and an assignment of the tasks to hierarchical levels of professional and paraprofessional personnel according to the training and ability required for efficient and effective performance. The submodel provides five professional, three paraprofessional, and adjunct and volunteer personnel levels in the vertical differentiation; it divides the school program into broad function areas of horizontal differentiation.

The Vertical Hierarchy—Professional Personnel

The five levels of professional personnel are the consulting teacher, directing teacher, staff teacher, instructor, and resident intern. These may be diagrammatically shown on a series of concentric circles, with the outer ring representing the highest level in the vertical hierarchy. This diagram is presented in Figure 1. These positions are ranked according to degrees of responsibility and accountability inherent in the tasks performed, including the level of training and amount of experience required, and the extent of the influence of the position. The job specifications of any of the five levels will depend upon the size and type of school to which the individual is assigned. In a small elementary school, for example,

FIGURE 1

The Total Vertical Hierarchy and Concomitant Positions in the System Model

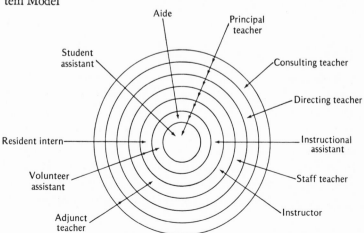

the budget process is much less complex than that of a large senior high school. A similar relationship of complexity exists in many of the tasks of the entire instructional program. A particular position, therefore, may exist in different numbers and have varying job specifications in different sizes or types of schools; or it may not be a part of the staff in some schools at all. The procedure for determining the number of a particular level of staff to be assigned to a school and the job specifications of each is presented in more detail in the section on the implementation submodel, which is presented later in this report.

Only the position of staff teacher is tenured, subject to the laws pertaining to tenure status. When promoted to a higher rank, a person who previously held tenure as a staff teacher would retain that status; and, if he reverts to the position of staff teacher, would resume the tenure.

Promotion may be from any position to any higher position, depending upon qualifications met. These are closely related to job specifications as discussed in a subsequent section. Selection for promotion may result from application or invitation.

Although the job specifications vary, each position has certain basic, inherent characteristics which distinguish it in the vertical hierarchy and constitute an operational definition.

The consulting teacher. The consulting teacher has major responsibility for leadership in a broad area of the instructional program. He may be responsible for supervising several grade levels, a particular discipline in several grade levels, coordinated disciplines in a school or grade level, or one or more of the function areas of instruction, staff development, planning-research-evaluation-reporting, or administration. He will have influence upon a large sector of the school population and will perform tasks at a level of sophistication sufficiently high to require maximum available training and talent. Generally he will not be in a position of direct line authority or implementation; but instead will provide developmental, consultative, and advisory services. His assignment to direct instruction and contact with students will be for less than full time, and will depend upon his specific job responsibilities.

The directing teacher. The directing teacher has major responsibility and accountability for leadership in a limited part of the instructional program. He may be the leader of a team, a grade level, or a department. He is responsible for a single discipline in one school, or may be assigned leadership responsibility in one of the function areas. He is in a direct-line authority position and is responsible for implementing a phase of the instructional program. He is a master practitioner who should be expert in at least one mode of instruction, discipline, or service area and should be knowledgeable in others. In small or less-complex school centers, he will provide services that otherwise would be provided by a consulting teacher. He will be assigned to direct instruction for approximately three-fourths of his time, unless assigned to duties basically administrative.

The staff teacher. The staff teacher is comparable to the traditional classroom teacher in classification but has sufficient experience to place him beyond a probationary period, usually three years. He is assigned to a team, to a single or unified discipline, or to duties in one of the function areas. In general, he will be assigned to full-time direct instruction. In very small schools, he may provide services otherwise provided by a directing or consulting teacher.

The instructor. The instructor is a beginning teacher who will undergo a probationary period, usually three years, before assignment to a higher classification. He will work closely with and assist the staff teachers or directing teachers.

He will be assigned to full-time direct instruction and will receive significant supervision and assistance, usually from a directing teacher. In some schools he may be assigned part of his duties in a function area other than direct instruction.

The resident intern. The resident intern is a college student in his final year of preservice training. He will be assigned full time for one year in direct instruction, but will be provided released time to participate in all activities required by his college. He will be assigned during the year to a staff teacher, a directing teacher, or a team for the day-to-day supervision appropriate to an internship.

The Vertical Hierarchy—Paraprofessional Personnel

The three levels of paraprofessional personnel are the instructional assistant, the aide, and the student assistant. These are diagrammatically shown in relation to the professional personnel in the hierarchy in Figure 1. These positions are ranked according to degrees of responsibility, training, and experience; and job specifications are developed according to the same procedures applied to the professional staff.

The instructional assistant. The instructional assistant is assigned to full-time direct instruction, but on a limited basis. He will perform instructional duties, usually under continual supervision and with a staff teacher or directing teacher. When not under immediate observation, the instructional assistant will perform only those instructional duties which are assigned by a professional teacher and which do not require professional training or permit decision making that affects the instructional program.

The aide. The teacher aide may be assigned duties that are essentially clerical, technical, or monitorial. He will assist a member of the professional staff by performing routine tasks requiring training of a vocational rather than professional nature. In some schools or departments, he may assist in the supervision of students under the direction of a professional teacher.

The student assistant.   The student assistant is a high school or area college student who is employed on a part-time basis and paid an hourly wage. He may perform any duties assigned to him by the teacher in charge of a team or department, or by another staff member designated by that leader. These duties may be similar to the aide's, or the student assistant may be assigned limited instructional tasks, such as helping individual or small groups of students with particular problems identified and described by a professional teacher.

The Vertical Hierarchy—Other Categories

The adjunct teacher.   The adjunct teacher is a lay person who possesses particular expertise in a certain field as a full-time practitioner or a retiree, or as a result of an avocation or special experience. This expertise may be in the arts, sciences, business, technology, or any field from which special knowledge is applicable at a given point in an instructional program. The adjunct is employed, usually on a daily-rate basis, to perform a specific task determined by the professional teacher or team responsible for the instruction to which the adjunct's knowledge is related. The adjunct may lecture to a group of students, give demonstrations or performances, or introduce students to some special skill on a group or individual basis. In every case, the work of the adjunct is pre-planned, and a part of the regular instructional program. The adjunct may be employed for any period of time and any number of times appropriate to the curriculum. He may be paid at the daily rate of any of the top four levels of the professional hierarchy, or at an honorarium otherwise determined.

The volunteer assistant. The utilization of adjunct teachers does not limit or preclude the use of volunteer assistance from lay persons. In some school centers, lay citizens may volunteer periodic or regular work in the schools in a capacity similar to that of instructional assistant, aide, or adjunct teacher. These may be persons who are not able to commit themselves to regular service or who do not care to be paid staff. The services of the volunteer assistant should be coordinated by the directing teacher.

The adjunct-teacher and the volunteer-assistant positions in the hierarchy are shown on the circular model in Figure 1.

The principal. The principal, or principal-teacher, is the one person in the school having ultimate legal or local responsibility for the overall instructional program of the school. In a school or school district in transition from traditional to differentiated staffing, the principal may fit into the system model either as the traditional final-authority figure, or as one of a board in the school, each of whom has an equal vote in school management decisions. In the latter situation, responsibility also would be shared and that condition officially recognized by the school system's legally governing body.

In a differentiated-staffing model with shared decision making, the principal will have the primary responsibility for causing the decisions of the faculty board to be carried out. He is responsible for seeing that the environment of the school is maximal for the instructional program. He is responsible for providing to the teachers who are engaged in direct instruction the facilities, equipment, materials, and organization necessary for instruction. The principal-teacher, as he would be called in a differentiated-staffing model, will be assigned to direct instruction of students in proportion to the time demands of the administrative job specifications determined by the size and type of school to which he is assigned.

The position of the principal-teacher is shown on the circular model of the complete vertical hierarchy in Figure 1.

The faculty board. The faculty board consists of the principal or principal-teacher, the consulting teachers, and the directing teachers of a school. If the staff of a school requests, one or more of the faculty other than those specified may be appointed to the faculty board for a specified period of time. This would be appropriate in schools in which a particular discipline or function area was not represented by a directing or consulting teacher, and where such representation was desirable.

The board is the governing body of the school. Within the limitation of law, school district policy, and district administrative regulations, the faculty board oversees the operation of the school and is the decision-making body in that center. Each member has one vote, and the principal may or may not possess veto power, as determined by law or local policy. As in traditional staffing patterns in which the principal may delegate certain authority to other members of the staff, the faculty board would normally be expected to delegate authority in a differentiated-staffing organization.

If a school system is substantially involved in differentiated staffing, a central board may be organized to coordinate the programs of individual schools in the school system. This board would be comprised of all principal-teachers and consulting or directing teachers in a small school system, or of delegates elected by each faculty board to represent the individual school. This representation would be proportional to the schools' enrollments.

In a school system in the early stages of differentiated-staffing implementation, a coordinating committee should be selected by and as representatives of the major personnel divisions of the school system, such as principals, elementary and secondary teachers, counselors, supervisors, central administrative staff, paraprofessionals, business services, and each other category of personnel. This central steering committee should be authorized by the school-system board of education and recognized as its official advisory agent on differentiated staffing.

In either a predominantly traditionally staffed or a differentiated-staffed school system, the final administrative authority remains with the superintendent. The ultimate legally constituted local authority remains with the board of education.

The Horizontal Differentiation—The Function Areas

An important principle of differentiated staffing involves the assignment of personnel to perform those tasks for which their training, experience, interest, and abilities best qualify them, rather than the more traditional assignment to teachers of responsibility for all parts of the teaching function in a particular course or class. This differentiation in the system model is based partly upon the vertical hierarchy of responsibility and accountability discussed in the section preceding. It is also based upon the division of the instructional program into tasks requiring different kinds of personnel qualifications at equivalent levels of responsibility and accountability, called horizontal differentiation.

In this model the total instructional program is divided into four broad function areas: instruction, staff development, administration, and planning-research-evaluation-reporting; and the tasks identified as essential to the operation of the program are classified into those four areas. This may be represented diagrammatically on the concentric-circle model of the vertical hierarchy as shown in Figure 2. In the diagram, the dotted lines are used to indicate that the relative scope of any of the four function areas is not absolute, but may vary among schools, and that the tasks in the instructional program may be classified in different broad-function areas.

The role of any of the professional or paraprofessional staff may exist in any of the function areas. In a particular size and type of school, the job specifications may provide for a consulting teacher in administration and in staff development, and for several in the area of instruction. In a smaller or less complex school center, job specifications may assign similar tasks to directing teachers in one or more of those areas. As stated earlier, this job-specification procedure, referred to earlier in the section on professional and paraprofessional staffs, is discussed in detail in a subsequent section of this report on the implementation submodel.

Horizontal differentiation within function areas. Within each function area, the differentiation among teachers of equal vertical status is developed further to assign tasks to staff members according to their abilities, training, experience, and interest. In the area of instruction, some teachers will perform best in large-group instruction; others will conduct seminars, supervise laboratories, or work with individual students in academic or counseling situations. In multidiscipline

FIGURE 2
Function Areas

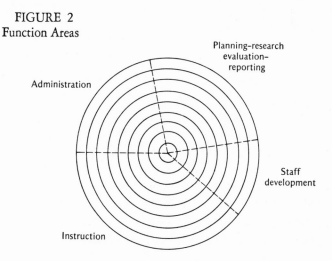

areas or nondepartmentalized organization, some teachers will be specialists in language arts or mathematics or social studies.

In the other function areas, similar differentiation of the staff assignments will be developed. In all areas, the professional and paraprofessional staff that comprises a team or other organizational unit, usually with a directing teacher, will be responsible for the horizontal differentiation. Staff should be selected to complete each organizational unit so that all of the needed abilities are present. Supervising the selection of new staff members according to the prescription of the existing team or unit is a responsibility of the faculty board. Efficient utilization of the personnel resources through horizontal differentiation is the continuing responsibility of the team or other organizational unit. Continual evaluation of the efficacy of the unit's horizontal differentiation is the responsibility of the directing teacher, working with the other staff members in the unit. If the horizontal differentiation is found to be less than optimum, reorganization can be undertaken at any time. If contractual or ethical commitments are not violated, even the vertical staffing can be changed. This responsiveness to changing needs of a particular instructional setting is the essence of the fluidity of the system model.

THE IMPLEMENTATION SUBMODEL

The implementation submodel is designed to give procedures by which each school may select autonomously the staffing pattern most appropriate for that school's instructional program and philosophy, while at the same time adhering to minimum school-system standards of consistency of allocation of resources, work loads, performance, and remuneration.

This submodel consists of the following sections:

1. A process for the allocation of total staff units to each school
2. The divison of all schools into seven classifications according to size and type
3. An assignment of unit values to each position in the vertical hierarchy of the staffing submodel
4. A procedure for determining the approximate recommended number of each job classification needed at a particular school
5. A set of charts from which job specifications may be collated for each staff member
6. The general criteria by which the staff is held accountable for performance

Allocation of Units

Staff units are allocated to each school according to a pupil-teacher ratio appropriate for the level of the school. This ratio will be determined by central-office administration according to the total funds available for instructional-personnel salaries, the average salary expected to be paid during the school year, and the resulting total number of instructional units available to the school system. For example, if 8,000,000 dollars is available for salaries and the average salary is 8,000 dollars, then 1,000 units can be allocated to schools in the district for the year.

The pupil-teacher ratio used to determine units may be the same for all schools, or a lower ratio may be used at some levels than at others. In either case, the number of pupils expected at a particular school is divided by the pupil-teacher ratio to determine the number of staff units assigned to that school. If the pupil-teacher ratio applied is 20 to 1, a school of 1000 pupils would be allocated 50 units.

In a school district that is entirely or predominantly staffed on a differentiated-staffing model, certain personnel services traditionally assigned to a central staff will be decentralized.

Examples of these include instructional supervisors and some business and buildings and grounds services. Where these are decentralized, the unit value of the services would be allocated to the schools in proportion to enrollments. These would be added as plus factors to school allocations where decentralization was only partial in a school system, but could be considered as part of the original unit allocation process in school systems in which all such services were decentralized.

Classification of Schools
All schools are classified into one of seven categories:

1. Elementary schools up to 300 pupils
2. Elementary schools with more than 300 pupils
3. Junior high schools up to 750 students
4. Junior high schools with more than 750 students
5. Senior high schools up to 1000 students
6. Senior high schools with more than 1000 students
7. School centers with grades kindergarten through 9 or higher

The first six classifications were determined by using for the larger classes the maximum elementary, junior high, and senior high school enrollments considered by the pilot school system to be desirable; and using half of those enrollments for the smaller classifications. Schools with enrollments very close to the dividing point might utilize the implementation procedures designed for either the smaller or larger classifications, choosing that which in the staff's judgment is more appropriate to the local philosophy and circumstances. Different classifications of the schools may be used by other school districts.

Unit Values of the Vertical Hierarchy
The autonomy of a school to select its staffing pattern and the adherence to standards of minimum consistency with school-

system unit allocations are coordinated through the selection of staff from the staffing submodel. Each position on that submodel is assigned a unit value, with the position of staff teacher equal to 1.00, and considered the index point to which each other position's unit value is related. These values are shown in Table 1.

The unit values of each position were determined by relating the cost of the median salary of that position to the mean salary of all instructional personnel. An appropriate salary schedule was prepared for each position, and the median salary on that schedule divided by the mean instructional salary. The results were rounded to the indexes shown in Table 1.

In the computation of the mean instructional salaries, all teachers on any step of the traditional salary schedule were included. Therefore, the index value of staff teacher and instructor are the same.

Procedure for Determining the Staffing Pattern

The implementation submodel is a procedure by which a school is staffed with the number of personnel at each position

TABLE 1
Unit Values of Staff Positions

Position	Unit Value	Number of Days of Service
Principal-teacher	1.50	222
Consulting teacher	1.50	211
Directing teacher	1.25	211
Staff teacher	1.00	196
Instructor	1.00	196
Resident intern	.50	190
Instructional assistant	.50	190
Aide	.35	190
Student assistant	.03	Per hour, 180 days
Adjunct	N/A	Separate budget
Volunteer	N/A	As volunteered

TABLE 2
Task-Responsibility Chart

Administration Elementary up to 300	Consulting Teacher	Directing Teacher	Staff Teacher
1. Providing budget data			
School-wide		P[a]	A
Team- or dept.-wide		A	P
Class-wide		A	P
2. Compiling data and preparing budget		P	A

3. Ordering and distributing
   supplies, materials and
   equipment
		P	A

4. Keeping student attendance		P	A
5. Supervising custodial and maintenance		P	
6. Supervising food services		P	
7. Preparing accreditation reports		P	M
8. Establishing forms and systems for data processing		P	A

9. Establishing forms and
   systems for data storage
   and dissemination
		A	A

10. Providing scheduling data			
School-wide		P	A
Team-wide		A	P
Class-wide		A	P
11. Scheduling		P	A
12. Inventorying materials and equipment		P	A

[a] P = Primary responsibility; M = Major responsibility; A = Assisting responsibility

on the hierarchy most appropriate to carry out the tasks of the instructional program in that school. In the staffing sub-model, the tasks were classified into four function areas: instruction, administration, planning-research-evaluation-reporting, and staff development. Each of these function areas has been subdivided into a series of broadly stated tasks to be performed, the totality of which constitutes the instructional program.

Instructor	Resident Intern	Instructional Assistant	Aides	Student Assistant
A	A	A	A	A
A	A	A	A	A
M	A	A	A	A
A	A	A	A	A
A	A	A	A	A
A	A	A	A	A
A	A	A	A	A
A	A			
A	A			
A	A			
A	A			
M	A	A	A	A
A	A			
A	A	M	A	A

The complexity of the tasks and the competency required to perform them vary among schools of different size or type. For each of the seven school classifications, a chart was prepared which lists the tasks in each function area and assigns responsibility for each task to one or more of the job classifications. One page of a sample chart is shown in Table 2, and represents approximately 20 percent of a complete chart for one classification of schools. A school's faculty board, or other group responsible for recommending a staffing pattern for that school, selects the appropriate task chart for that size and type of school and collates the tasks assigned as primary or major responsibility for each position on the vertical hierarchy. According to the number and kinds of these tasks, the faculty board determines how many of each staff position and what horizontal differentiation within each level the school needs for an optimum instructional program. They may then use their allocated units for the recommended staff.

Job-Specification Charts

The charts directly provide the job specifications for each position on the vertical hierarchy. Each task is assigned as a major, primary, or assisting responsibility. Primary responsibility and accountability is defined as that of causing a task to be undertaken and completed. Major responsibility and accountability is defined as that of performing a task. Assisting responsibility is that of assisting in a task when requested by the person who has primary responsibility.

The job specifications of any one person may not include all of the tasks shown in the column for the particular position on the vertical hierarchy. The tasks may be horizontally differentiated and comprehensive enough to be assigned to several staff members at that same vertical level during the process of determining the staffing pattern of the school. The job specifications of any one staff member are the collection of tasks from the column in the chart that is appropriate for his qualifications and time assignment.

For example, in Table 2 broad tasks are listed for the staff of an elementary school of up to 300 enrollment. The complete chart would list 12 tasks in the area of administration; in curriculum, 5; in instruction, 7; in research-planning-evaluation-reporting, 5; and in staff development, 2. Some of these are subdivided into school-wide, team, or class responsibilities. The first task shown—providing budget data, school-wide—is assigned as a primary responsibility for a directing teacher, assisted by those in all of the other staff positions. In the absence of the assignment of primary or major responsibility for any one task, both responsibilities are included in the one assigned. To determine the complete job of one or more directing teachers, the persons responsible for staffing a school would collate all of the primary and major responsibilities in the directing-teacher column of the chart and decide the appropriate number of people and the kinds of training needed to perform all those tasks. The same process is repeated for each column representing one of the staff positions, and the same process applies to the job-specification charts for each of the seven classifications of schools.

In Table 3 a comparison is presented of the assignment of one sample task to various levels of personnel in each .of the seven classifications of schools. The assignment of primary and major responsibility shifts from one staff position to another in different-sized schools.

The faculty board representing each school may deviate one

TABLE 3

Comparison of a Sample Task[a] Assignment to Staff in Schools of Various Sizes and Types

School size and Type	C.T.[b]	D.T.	S.T.	Ins.	R.I.	I.A.	Aide	S.A.
Elementary, up to 300	—	M[c]	P	M	A	A	A	A
Elementary, more than 300	M	P	M	A	A	A	A	A
Junior high, up to 750	M	P	M	A	A	A	A	A
Junior high, more than 750	M	P	M	A	A	A	A	A
Senior high, up to 1,000	M	P	M	A	A	A	A	A
Senior high, more than 1000	P	M	A	A	A	A	A	A
Kindergarten to grade 12	P	M	A	A	A	A	A	A

[a] Writing curriculum from basic objectives-courses of study

[b] C.T.: consulting teacher; D.T.: directing teacher; S.T.: staff teacher; Ins.: instructor; R.I.: resident intern; I.A.: instructional assistant; Aide: teacher's aide; S.A.: student assistant

[c] M: Major responsibility; P: Primary responsibility; A: Assisting responsibility

column, or staff position, in either direction in the assignment of any task to a position on the vertical hierarchy. In this manner, a task assigned to a directing teacher on the chart for that size and type school may be reassigned to a staff teacher or a consulting teacher if, in the opinion of the faculty board, that change improves the individual school's staff organization. The deviation increases the autonomy of a school to design its staffing pattern, while the limitation on the deviation from the charts assures minimum consistency with school-system job specifications. The permitted deviation also provides the school a means of adjusting its staffing pattern to fit within the total allocated units, while assuring that staff is provided for all appropriate tasks.

The job specifications also provide criteria to assist in the screening and selection of staff, and for the development of in-service education programs. The credentials and results of the interview of a candidate provide a selection committee or administrator with evidence to compare to the job specification of the position. The necessary qualifications of the candidate are essentially inherent in the job specifications. The kinds of experience and training of the candidate which are directly related to job specifications are the major selection criteria. A particular degree or length of experience is not required at any job level. When employed, the in-service experiences qualify the teacher.

Criteria of Accountability

The job specification charts are prepared, modified, and updated by a central ad hoc curriculum committee. The tasks listed in those charts are inclusive of the total instructional program of the school system. A particular school may select autonomously a staffing pattern different from a comparable school, but each is responsible for providing an instructional program that includes the specification of the job charts, board of education policies, accreditation standards, and state laws and regulations.

The evaluation of an individual staff member is based upon the job specifications. The performance of those tasks which are behaviorally stated may be objectively evaluated by observation of the extent of the performance according to the criteria inherent in the specifications. Performance of other tasks will be evaluated more subjectively, but based also upon the job specifications. Both kinds of evaluation will be conducted by all persons who constitute a particular instructional team or staff grouping; thus, evaluation of an individual's performance is by subordinates, peers, and superiors.

STAFFING PATTERN FOR A
SELECTED JUNIOR HIGH SCHOOL

Venice Junior High School is located in Venice, Florida, in Sarasota County. It housed grades 7, 8, and 9, with a 1970–1971 second-month enrollment of 834. It had been allocated 44.7 staff units, based upon a student-teacher ratio of approximately 20 to 1. Utilizing the procedures of the implementation submodel and selecting a staff from the staffing submodel, the faculty board of the school proposed the staffing pattern for the 1970–1971 school year shown in Table 4. Table 4 also shows the staffing pattern that would have been used in a traditional organization in that school in 1970–1971. Table 5 compares the 1970–1971 instructional salary costs by departments and total faculty of the differentiated-staffing model with the traditional organization.

Scheduling of the Students

The differentiated-staffing pattern at Venice Junior High School was based upon the task analysis described preceding. It reflected the staff's understanding that different modes of instruction must be provided to approach the efficiency and

TABLE 4
Comparison of Traditional and Differentiated Staffing Patterns at Venice Junior High School

Department	Traditional Staffing, Number of Teachers	Differentiated Staffing
English	7	1 Directing teacher 4 Staff teachers 1 Instructor 2 Aides
Mathematics	6	1 Directing teacher 2 Staff teachers 1 Instructor 1 Instructional assistant 1.5 Aides 8 Student assistants— 1 hr./day
Science	6	1 Directing teacher 4 Staff teachers 2 Aides 1 Student assistant
Social Studies	6	1 Directing teacher 2 Staff teachers 2 Instructors 2 Aides
Physical Education	5	1 Directing teacher 4 Staff teachers
Foreign Language	3 plus 2 part-time	1 Directing teacher 3 Staff teachers 1.5 Aides
Electives	6 plus 2 part-time	1 Directing teacher 2 Staff teachers 2 Part-time staff teachers 3 Instructors 1.5 Aides
Instructional Media	1 part-time	1 Part-time directing teacher 1 Staff teacher 3 Aides
Counseling	2	1 Staff teacher
Administration	1 Principal 1 Assistant principal	1 Principal 1 Directing teacher (research-evaluation-staff development)

TABLE 5

Comparison of Salary Costs at Venice Junior High School, 1970–1971, Second Month

Department	Traditional	Differentiated
English	$60,932	$58,260
Mathematics	51,356	49,350
Science	55,546	54,320
Social Studies	48,226	46,490
Physical Education	44,820	47,395
Foreign Language	37,733	40,955
Electives	50,556	58,180
Instructional Media, Counseling, and Administration	63,600	63,036
Total staff	$412,769	$417,986

flexibility needed to optimize learning for the individual student. The staff needed the organizational capability to schedule students into large groups, seminars, or individually for particular learning experiences. According to the student's need and the subject area, even daily changes in any schedule might be necessary. In addition, a common planning time for the staff members in each department was needed daily in order to discuss, diagnose, and prescribe for the dynamic instructional needs of the students. Finally, the staff believed that every student must be *accountable to some teacher or department* at all times during the day; even though the student might be assigned to or permitted to choose a different activity, the teacher or department to which he was scheduled remained responsible for the student.

The schedule designed was a simple grouping of the student body into six sections, each comprising one-half of each of the three grades and numbering approximately 140 students. Table 6 shows the basic scheduling of each of the six groups, with explanatory material following.

TABLE 6
The Venice Junior High School, 1970–1971 Schedule

	1	2	3	4		5	6	7	8
Major Departments									
English	9A	8A	Plan	7A	Lunch	9B	8B	Plan	7B
Math	7A	Plan	8A	9A	Lunch	7B	Plan	8B	9B
Science	Plan	7A	9A	8A	Lunch	Plan	7B	9B	8B
Social Studies	8A	9A	7A	Plan	Lunch	8B	9B	7B	Plan
Other Departments									
Conglomerate	8B &	7B &	7B &	Plan	Lunch	8A &	7A &	7A &	
and For. Lang.	9B	9B	8B	Plan	Lunch	9A	9A	8A	
Phys. Educ.	7B	8B	9B	Plan	Lunch	7A	8A	9A	

The following points will serve to expand the data given in Table 6:

1. 8A (for example) is simply a notation of half of grade 8. It does not suggest grouping or academic level.
2. The Conglomerate Department includes industrial arts, home economics, art, music, typing, and study hall (un-scheduled time).
3. The four major subjects and physical education are required of all students all three years.
4. Each student is required to take at least one year of industrial arts (boys) or home economics (girls), one course in art, one course in music, and one course in foreign language some time in junior high.
5. The major department periods are 45 minutes, the others 55 minutes. Passing time is 3 minutes.
6. During the time that a student is scheduled to a *major* department, that staff may assign him to any combination of blocks of time within the 45 minutes to large-group, seminar, or individual instruction on any given day. This is completely determined by that department, and is planned and announced as far in advance as practical and instructionally sound. Each major department has two

45-minute planning periods together every day to make this joint planning possible.

7. In the Conglomerate Department, a student may be scheduled for a full 55-minute period of one of the related subjects, or may be taking two such subjects for shorter "periods-within-periods." In the Conglomerate Department, study hall, or resource time, is scheduled as a major subject.

8. There is no purposely scheduled full-time periods for students. There may be a few minutes of "dead" time for an individual caused by imperfect overlapping of the major departments' eight periods and the other departments' seven periods. These periods of time are few and brief, and the student is not directly supervised during those times.

9. At any other time that a student is permitted free time, regardless of where he goes, he is the responsibility of the department to which he was scheduled.

10. The major departments may stagger the lunch periods to include part of periods 4 and 5.

11. Through mutual agreement, any two departments may exchange all or some students, or reverse schedules. For example, if the English and mathematics departments agreed in advance, the 8A students could remain in English during periods 2 and 3 while the mathematics department had double planning time. The situation would be reversed later to make up time. This permits easy scheduling of long films, field trips, staff conferences and intermixture of grades for ability and achievement grouping.

EVALUATION

Evaluation, to be meaningful, must be based upon clearly defined objectives. Unless expectations from an innovation are specified in advance, the effectiveness of the program cannot be determined.

The objectives of differentiated staffing should be both immediate and long-range. The ultimate or long-range objective is the improvement of learning for the individual student. It is unlikely that significant change in learning can be demonstrated and attributed to differentiated staffing in one or two years. However, long-range evaluation must be based upon a comparison with preinnovation achievement. Thus, base-line data should be collected when the program is begun.

More immediate evaluation of the effect of differentiated staffing on the organization of the schools is possible. During the first year of operation, evaluators can observe whether or not the properties attributed to the local differentiated-staffing model are working. Does it provide the possibility for a teacher to earn higher salaries without leaving the classroom; an increased share in decision making by teachers; greater flexibility and individualization in the use of facilities, time, and curriculum; assignment of staff to tasks commensurate with their training and experience; and improved attitude toward the school by students, community, and staff. Each of these can be measured in tangible or even quantifiable terms such as dollars paid, staff time spent in specific tasks, attendance rates, use of the library and other resources, what decisions are made and by whom, changes in curriculum, and the variety of instructional modes utilized. Each of these can be compared to related data about earlier practices.

During the 1970–1971 school year, the evaluation of the Venice Junior High School program included all of these components. Independent evaluations were conducted by university consultants, the school staff, the Sarasota County Teachers Association, central office administration, the U.S. Office of Education, the Florida State Department of Education, and a doctoral student whose dissertation topic was the evaluation of the model. In addition, outside visitors were asked to evaluate the program using an instrument prepared by the doctoral student. All of these findings were combined to provide a comprehensive judgment of the first year of operation. Similar evaluation will continue throughout the developmental years of the program. The findings of all evaluations were presented to the school board, the community, and other interested groups.

SOME PROBLEMS AND RECOMMENDATIONS

Early in the first year of operation of the staffing model described above, two major problems were apparent: the need for further refinement of staff roles, or job specifications, and the need for in-service training to improve human relations and develop a flexible individualized curriuclum.

Detailed task analyses of the instructional program, based upon objectives stated in terms of learner behavior, should be developed to form the basis for the design of staff-differentiation models. These behavioral objectives may be stated differently in various school systems, but a process of task analysis that can be commonly applied is needed.

Preservice and in-service education programs should be designed and implemented to prepare teachers and paraprofessionals for roles in a differentiated-staffing organization. These training programs should include components on task analysis, design of models, implementation mechanics, the human relations of teaching in hierarchical teams, curriculum development and modification, design of resource or materials centers, procedures of operation in flexibly sized groups, and flexible scheduling of time and material resources.

Finally, it is suggested that school districts involved or interested in the concept of differentiated staffing begin to call it something else.

model
C

Mesa, Arizona

Introduction

Of all the models the author has knowledge of, the Arizona-Mesa Differentiated Staffing project must be considered one of the most innovative. The project staff, headed by Fenwick English, who formerly served as project director for the Temple City project, has added two new dimensions to an already innovative idea. First, no permanent hierarchy of positions has been established. The approach used is to tie the hierarchy to the objectives to be achieved. A group of teachers organize themselves into a hierarchical team to accomplish a particular objective or objectives. When the objectives have been achieved and are no longer valid, the team disbands or reorganizes to achieve a new objective. Second, performance contracting will be utilized. Through the board of education a series of *request for proposal* (RFP), which specify the objectives to be achieved, are sent to the schools with requests for "bids." The staff, as teams or as individuals, submit bids on one or more RFPs. The bids specifies, among other things, the cost of achieving the objectives of an RFP. The bids are negotiated through the board of education.

When the RFP is completed, the results are evaluated. Depending on the results of the evaluation, the team may receive the amount bid, be penalized, or receive incentives. These are obviously innovative ideas which merit serious consideration and thorough investigation.

As was the case with the Sarasota County report, the choice of the Arizona-Mesa project proved to be a most fortuitous one. Included in the Arizona-Mesa report are some excellent examples of a systematic approach to planning. Although the planning models may not have direct application in other situations, they should provide some insight into the planning process and how it might be approached. Figures 4 and 5 should be particularly valuable for school districts in the preplanning stage but may also prove helpful for those at the planning stage. The Project PERT (program evaluation and review technique), Figure 4, and the accompanying task analysis are exceptionally well done. A careful analysis of this material will demonstrate the sharp break with traditional planning procedures. No one can predict whether a particular innovative idea will prove to be successful, but planning, as conceived in the Project PERT and task analysis, will enormously increase the chances of success. The power of this planning strategy can be seen in the Temple City project, which was planned in this way and seems well on its way to succeeding.

THE ARIZONA-MESA DIFFERENTIATED STAFFING PROJECT: DIFFERENTIATED STAFFING: GENERATION TWO

Fenwick W. English, George N. Smith, and James K. Zaharis

The main thrust of the Mesa project is to prove the feasibility of a different conceptual base for a differentiated-staffing hierarchy.[1] The premise is that a static or unchanging hierarchy of teaching roles cannot be based on the need of pupils, since if needs change (as they will if instruction is effective), roles too must enjoy the capacity of change. The Mesa approach is to create a new fluid model whereby teaching roles are defined by particular pupil needs in a particular school building. When these needs are met, through a *performance contract*, the roles end.

Teaching tasks are related to pupil needs via an ongoing

[1] Adapted from a description of the Arizona-Mesa project which appeared in SPU-LTI Newsletter, Amherst, Mass.: University of Massachusetts, School of Education, January 1971, pp. 3–4.

assessment of pupil needs. Roles are differentiated horizontally, but they do not assume a hierarchy until a specific set of objectives, the learning situation, and time allotment are established. The scheme also allows for the formation and re-formation of various subhierarchies. At the expiration of the time allotment, any ranking of position reverts to a horizontal plane until a new set of objectives in a new time allotment has been negotiated and accepted by all parties.

The parameters of the Mesa model were developed under the seasoning of the previous five years of development of the concept in California and elsewhere. The major flaw with static hierarchies of differentiated roles is that one must assume that student needs are just as static, if any claim is made that teacher behavior is aimed at client (student) need. If no claim is made, then we have a solution to a teacher problem which may, in fact, run contrary to the purpose of creating a more humane institution for learning. Early models of staff differentiation merely extended the same assumptions of staffing of the traditional schools and assumed that the solution to the problem of a career ladder was to copy the administrative career ladder. This was done by tacking onto established roles additional responsibilities which created differentiated staffing but had little to do with differentiating instruction in the school. New roles were principally concerned with keeping teachers in the profession. Questions regarding what kind of behavior was being rewarded and encouraged were not asked. The Mesa approach does not aim to perpetuate this short-lived tradition.

Two major innovative concepts will appear in any models developed by the respective faculties.

1. The models derived from the staffs contain a fluid vertical relationship among the roles that fluctuate in relation to the instructional objectives for students and a specific

FIGURE 1
Horizontal Differentiation: Student Goal Defined, Phase I

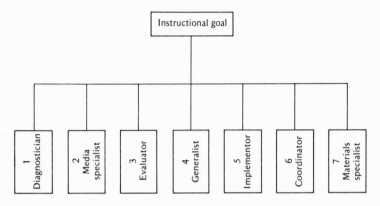

time allotment established in a performance contract.

In this phase (Figure 1) the instructional goals are defined, and the staff determines the expertise and skills necessary to accomplish the student goal. This is horizontal differentiation, and the skills can be secured from within the organization; or if the professional team believe they do not possess these skills, they can go outside the organization.

In this phase (Figure 2) the teaching teams determine which of the skills are most important in order to reach this specific student goal. The tasks are then arranged in a vertical relationship in order to successfully complete this particular student goal. After this goal has been completed, the vertical staff differentiation returns to a horizontal differentiation.

This is the fluid hierarchy. By having fluidity we do not presuppose, in order to support a fixed series of positions, that we know what student needs will always be or that they will ever be static over a period of time. This remains the Achilles heel of fixed models of staff differentiation to date. However, we do admit that there will be certain organizational functions, such as coordination, diagnosis, prescription,

FIGURE 2

Vertical Differentiation: Goal to Develop a Reading Program for Slow Readers, Phase II

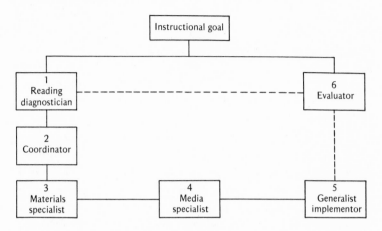

teaching, and evaluation, which must be carried out regardless of students or objectives. What makes these roles relevant will be their intertwining with specific tasks, and it is only through relating them to a set of prescribed time conditions and resources that role ranking assumes much meaning to the recipients of organizational behavior.

2. The concept of performance contracting and bidding for the resources of the organization with the board of education will be entered into by the teaching teams or the school boards with their administrative staffs. The resources will be allocated on the basis of solving specified student objectives.

There is no Mesa model of staff differentiation. There is a generic process by which any school staff builds its own from pupil objectives and its own resources. If a staffing model exists, it is time-specific and rooted to desired outcomes. When these conditions have been met, the model is abolished. Salary assumes a similar fluid base, as in the case of other professions, where pay may indeed fluctuate from month to month, depending on how much responsibility the professional in question desires and is able to assume. The managerial branch of the organization should move from a consideration of input (salary schedules) to output considerations (pupil behaviors). If teachers are productive and happy with a rigidly equalitarian pay mechanism and output specifications are met, the type of salary mechanism should be irrelevant to the board and administration. If teachers are not satisfied, then a new type of structure should be created. It is when performance output requirements are not met that procedures and mechanisms for salary should be reexamined. An example of how this actually works in practice is shown in Figure 3 and Table 1. In Figures 1 and 2, certain general roles are shown and then rearranged as student needs are diagnosed and related to required tasks. Table 1 and Figure 3 illustrate how specific objectives are related to a set of tasks and then to a hierarchical role structure. It is important to note that the tasks are set within a given time allotment. The function of the time allotment is to be able to arrange existing resources in a corresponding order based upon pupil needs. When needs are met, the role structure is abolished and a new one established which is set within a new time allotment. Thus, ranking of roles and tasks closely parallels pupil needs. Teaching tasks assume both an ordering in terms of sequence and a magnitude (need) based upon student priorities. The model of differentiated staffing is both client-centered and flexible and has the capacity to undergo alteration as pupil needs change with instruction. The model shown in Figure 3 and Table 1 emanated from an actual elementary school in Mesa.[2]

2 Phelps Wilkins, Jay Johnson, William Draper, Verna Baker, and Connie Bickford, "Proposal for Support in Research and Related Activities to Complete the Holmes School Needs Assessment and Differentiated Staffing Projects," mimeographed, Mesa Public Schools, Mesa, Arizona, November 1970, 11 pp.

FIGURE 3
Implementation of Program

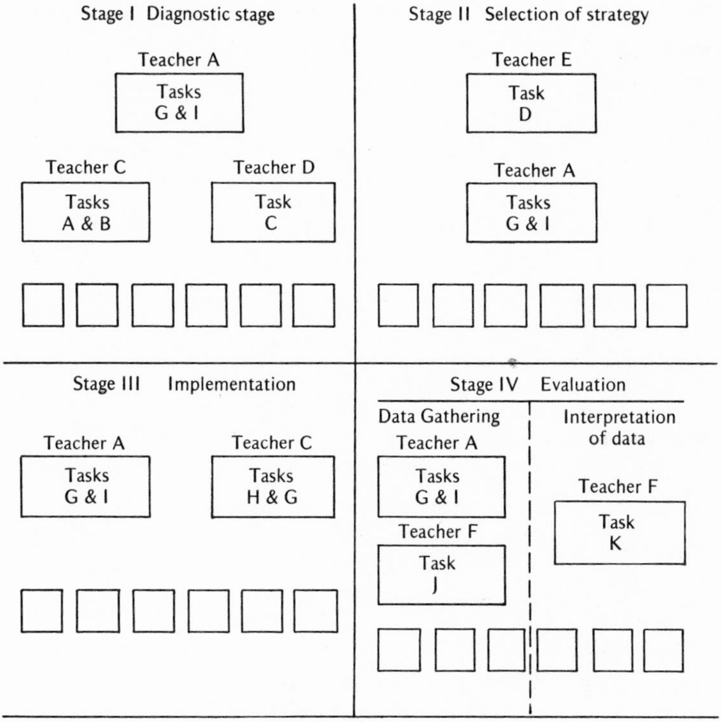

	Stage I Diagnostic stage		Stage II Selection of strategy
	Teacher A		Teacher E
	Tasks G & I		Task D
	Teacher C	Teacher D	Teacher A
	Tasks A & B	Task C	Tasks G & I

Stage III Implementation		Stage IV Evaluation	
		Data Gathering	Interpretation of data
Teacher A	Teacher C	Teacher A	
Tasks G & I	Tasks H & G	Tasks G & I	Teacher F
		Teacher F	Task K
		Task J	

Role Analysis

Role	Individual	Stage(s)	Position in hierarchy[a]
Diagnostician	Tea. C	I	Level 2
Coordinator	Tea. A	I, II, III, IV	I-1 II-2 III-1 IV-1
Researcher	Tea. E	II	Level 1
Strategist	Tea. E	II & III	II-1 III-1
Implementor	Tea. E, Staff	III	Teacher E– level 1 Other teachers – level 2
Evaluator	Tea. F	IV	Data gathering – Level 2 Interpretation – Level 1

[a] Position indicated by arabic numerals

TABLE 1

Planning for Identification and Achieving Objectives

I. IDENTIFIED NEED

- A. *What is:* 50% of students are reading at least one year below grade level.
- B. *What should be:* 80% of students should be reading within one year of grade level.
- C. *Measurable discrepancy:* 30% of students scored outside tolerances.

II. OBJECTIVES

- A. At the end of 150 days of instruction 80% or more of the students will score within one year of their grade level on the *Gates-McGintee* reading test.
- B. At the end of 150 days students in grades 4 to 6 will score 85 or better on *Holmes Reading Attitude Inventory.*

III. TASKS TO BE PERFORMED

- A. Identification of students scoring outside of tolerances
- B. Selection and administration of diagnostic skills test to target group
- C. Identification of students with sight, hearing, visual-perception problems, or the like
- D. Selection of strategies to be used to meet specific skill deficiencies
- E. Ordering materials and supplies
- F. Large and small group instruction
- G. Grouping and scheduling of students
- H. Periodic evaluation (30 days)
- I. Coordination of above activities
- J. Selection and administration of evaluative instruments
- K. Interpretation of evaluation data

IV. TEACHERS SELECTED FROM DIRECTORY TO PERFORM INDICATED TASKS

Teacher A

| *Skills* |
| [a]Coordinating |
| [a]Scheduling |
| inquiry method |
| [a]Small-group instruction |

Teacher B

| *Skills* |
| Art |
| Music |
| Writing objective |
| [a]Small-group instruction |

Teacher C

| *Skills* |
| [a]Knowledgeable in diagnostic |
| instruments |
| [a]Small-group instruction |

Teacher D

| *Skills* |
| Public relations |
| [a]Small-group instruction |
| [a]Visual perception |

Teacher E

| *Skills* |
| [a]Experienced reading teacher |
| [a]Media specialist |
| [a]Small-group instruction |

Teacher F

| *Skills* |
| [a]Knowledgeable in evaluative instruments |
| [a]Small-group instruction |
| [a]Large-group instruction |

[a] Skills needed to perform tasks listed in Part III

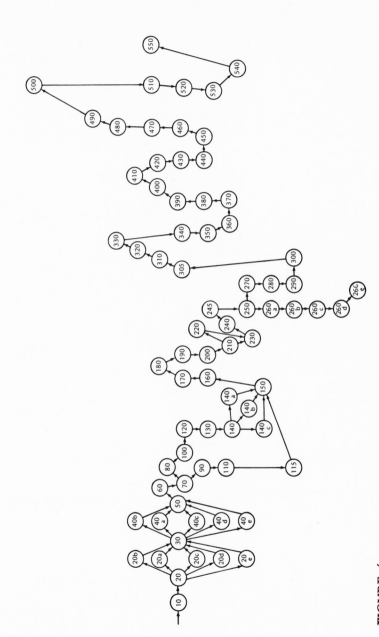

FIGURE 4
Project PERT Arizona-Mesa Differentiated-Staffing Consortium

PLANNING AND IMPLEMENTATION

Planning in the early phases of any project, and especially this project, are critical. The more involvement of people affected by the project, the better the possible chance for success in the final phases of the project. The PERT chart (Figure 4) indicates the sequential steps that are or will be taken in order to plan and implement the project.

Number	Task
10	Full-flow communication to all schools in the consortium on project purpose and preliminary information on differentiated staffing
20	Initial contacts by project staff with the following groups soliciting position papers on differentiated staffing: a. Representative teacher groups b. Arizona School Boards Association c. Arizona Taxpayers Association d. Arizona Parent-Teacher Association e. Appropriate elected officials, representatives, and agencies
30	Position papers collated into one joint statement
40	Position papers resubmitted to agencies for approval a. Representative teacher groups b. Arizona School Boards Association c. Arizona Taxpayers Association d. Arizona Parent-Teacher Association e. Appropriate elected officials, representatives, and agencies
50	Joint statement redrafted and distributed to staff with invitation to voluntarily join the project advisory committee
60	Teacher Advisory Committee formed to draft goals and procedures and to form task forces
70	Information packages prepared with taped slide presentation
80	Procedures for school application and criteria developed by project staff with the Teacher Advisory Committee

Number	Task
90	Paraprofessional criteria developed with appropriate Office of Economic Opportunity agency
100	Information packages distributed to school staffs; taped slide presentation shown to all schools in consortium areas
110	Screening for paraprofessional positions
115	Paraprofessionals selected for general training
120	Schools apply to be pilot models in differentiated staffing
130	School applications judged by Teachers Advisory Committee, project staff, and steering committee; pilot schools selected
140	Preliminary data gathered from pilot schools for needs assessment a. Community data b. Staff data (background, attitudes, etc.) c. Pupil data
150	Pilot-school staffs receive half-pay in-depth project orientation with selected paraprofessionals
160	Criteria developed by Teachers Advisory Council, staff and Steering Committee for Teacher Selection in summer institute from pilot schools; applications developed
170	Teachers in pilot schools apply for summer training; screening committee selected candidates and alternates
180	Performance criteria for summer institute developed
190	Criteria evaluated by Teachers Advisory Council and staff
200	Consultants and lecturers contacted and scheduled
210	Summer institute training modules developed
220	Pretests administered to trainees
230	Summer session begins (Table 2)
240	Summer training institute ends
245	Posttests administered to trainees
250	Preliminary differentiated-staffing models printed (Figure 5)
260	First progress report to consortium and position paper participants a. Representative teacher groups b. Arizona School Boards Association

    c. Arizona Taxpayers Association
    d. Arizona Parent-Teacher Association
    e. Appropriate elected officials, representatives, and agencies

TABLE 2
Training-Program Schedule

Week					
I	Introduction to training program and the system approach	System approach design to instruction	Diagramming ends-means exercises	Critique final problem	Introduction to curriculum-instruction performance objectives
II	Curriculum design Bloom's taxonomies	Work with curriculum consultants on miniunits	Critique of miniunits pre- and post-design	Miniunits	Evaluation of miniunits
III	DS model building	Model components	Roles	Role-simulation critique	Final models
IV	Contracting cost analysis	Bidding	Bidding	Tentative 1st-quarter contracts	Critique
V	Group dynamics analysis of people, problems, curriculum, roles	Problem identification	Skills	Application	Application critique
VI	Media units, media	Media	Media	Media	Media

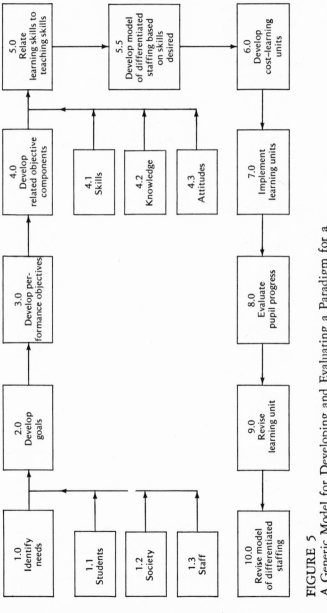

FIGURE 5
A Generic Model for Developing and Evaluating a Paradigm for a
Differentiated Staffing Based upon Identified Learner Needs

Number	Task
270	Report on models developed by staff in summer workshop
280	Summer reports distributed to all staff members in consortium
290	Teachers in pilot schools implement differentiated-staffing models, September 1970
300	Monthly progress meetings with pilot schools and project staff to troubleshoot
305	First comprehensive evaluation of staff and pupil progress
310	First major overhaul of staffing models by pilot schools during 1-week staff workshops in December
320	Pilot-school staffs propose to board of education procedures for performance contracting
330	Board reviews proposed procedures and recommends changes
340	Procedures adopted for first simulation
350	Board sets provisions of simulated contracts in previously agreed on subject areas
360	Pilot-school staffs simulate performance criteria and working relations with the board of education
370	Pilot-school staffs conduct performance contracts using differentiated staffing and related school subsystems Administer pretests to students
380	Performance contracts finished Students posttested Test results analyzed
390	Report submitted to the board of education on student performance
400	Major teacher, pupil, and parent critique and report on the board of education
410	Second major overhaul (models, roles, procedures, etc.)
420	Preliminary second summer institute objectives formulated from #410
430	Objectives approved by board and Teachers Advisory Council
440	Pilot-school staff teachers selected for institute
450	Summer consultants contacted

Number	Task
460	Second summer institute commences
	Pretests administered to trainees
470	Specific training modules initiated
480	Conclusion of summer institute
490	Posttests administered
500	Final models, roles, procedures developed for approval by the board of education
510	Board approves #500
520	Board writes first-performance student contracts for first semester
530	Teachers work with board on #520
540	Contracts accepted
550	Teachers plan and initiate contracts in September

DEALING WITH PRECEDENT: THE MYTH OF LINEARITY

American school systems are founded on principles of learning and teaching which are incompatible with one another. Learning is subordinated to teaching. Learning is highly personal, irregular, and elusive. When it became necessary to institutionalize it and to make it predictable for administrative convenience, much of the zest for learning vanished on the part of students.

In short, American education has developed around a concern for teaching and order. The appeal of the Quincy graded school over earlier one-room school houses and the Lancastrian model was its concern with developing criteria for creating pupil homogeneity for teaching ease via instructional uniformity. One-room schools with multiaged pupils presented visible evidence of pupil heterogeneity and pointed out rather clearly the fallacies of group-based instruction. With that difference removed by age-grading, group-based instruction became tenable, and pupils could be programmed annually.

Once educators convinced themselves that an important pupil difference was being dealt with, it was easy to begin building an organizational system which could be established by annual accruals of credits. The myth was enshrined, and we could get on with the business of teaching. It was all so very neat and predictable.

This concept of school may be called the "myth of *linearity*," and it led to the practice of dealing with students in blocks, a system of teacher training, and a whole set of biases about what was "educational" and a "good school." Linearity became a kind of educational rhetoric which we have learned to live by, sanction and legitimize by means of the credentialing process. School systems today are linear channels by which students move automatically down instructional assembly lines. A whole host of supertechnology has been created to streamline the process, and we have created subsystems to deal with those students and a few teachers who cannot "adjust to the system."

At the point of conceptualization of the teacher's role somewhere around 1848, society was considerably less complex. The teaching semiprofession had few real skills. A very low level of training was necessary along with a very low level of knowledge about any discipline or the learning process. As our knowledge of learning has expanded and our development of technology mushroomed, we have chosen to rationalize and use them within the old assumptions regarding learning as a linear phenomenon rather than use them as a base for changing them. We have selected refinement instead of reform. We have consistently failed to recognize the *iatrogenic situation,* that is, in the process of treating the patient, we have caused him to become increasingly ill. We have used our technology and knowledge to do better that which is fallacious and unjustified in the first place. We have legitimated precedent by reinforcing it, and we have found convenient rationalizations when our biases produced further illnesses on the part of students.

Performance contracting as a vehicle to provide incentives for the system to do better what it does now would be an absurdity, but that is precisely what is happening. In many cases we will have developed a more rigorous procedure than before for producing pupil anomie and disengagement. Performance contracting as an end in itself will be a first-class educational disaster.

PERFORMANCE CONTRACTING AS A REFORM: RECOGNIZING AND REWARDING DIVERSITY OR CREATING THE NONLINEAR SYSTEM

The value of performance contracting is that it provides a potent incentive for reform if it becomes conceptualized as a means by which:

1. The myth of linearity is shattered and replaced by dealing with pupils as individuals
2. It establishes a method for a reward system which recognizes pupil outcomes in keeping with their interests and potential, and provides a self-renewing basis for maintaining institutional sensitivity
3. It can become a device for the continued growth of the teaching profession and form a basis for responsible self-governance of the profession
4. The public may ascertain the profession's responsibility to perform the functions bestowed by society on it and an index of *pupil benefits* derived thereof

Envisioned, not as a tool by which pupils are compressed further into homogeneous masses via the establishment of airtight norms, but as a means to accompany educational reform, performance contracting offers the promise of a new reward structure which can provide a powerful stimulus to educational reform. Indeed, much of our problem now is that the incentive system in schools is impervious to pupil and teacher differences. Differences are talked about, but all is operationally sacrificed to preserve the necessary structural linearity.

Performance contracting can aid in the search for instructional alternatives by teachers for dealing effectively with pupil differences. It can be the method by which linearity is not reinforced and by which professional self-governance assumes a realistic base and is related to pupil benefits. A monolithic educational bureaucracy with its power elite decision-making structure is a natural outgrowth of a linear system. Both are functionally compatible. By changing the reward structure we create a *dysfunctional situation*. In the past we have attempted to innovate without changing the reward structure. Bluntly, we have not put our money where our mouth was. We have not rewarded diversity. Our efforts have gone into making the system work better. It is not surprising that a decade and several billion dollars later, we have not changed much of education in the classroom where it counts. We have deliberately avoided changing those variables which make a difference, that is, personnel and the personnel reward structure, which is both the salary system and the status and advancement (promotion) policies of the schools. The most important and fundamental promise of performance contracting is that it provides the rationale by which the educational reward structure which is based on assumptions of learning linearity may be radically altered. It can serve as a powerful means of forcing school systems to become client-centered for the first time. Similarly, it is horrifying to consider the idea as a means for merely reinforcing the status quo.

THE MESA MODEL: COMBINING
ACCOUNTABILITY, GOVERNANCE, AND REFORM

The Mesa approach to performance contracting is based upon the following assumptions:

1. That contracting is a logical step towards reinforcing a total thrust for reform, establishing a remunerative scheme which is responsive to the student and which is regulated by professional self-governance and the public represented in the school board; that there is a built-in compatibility between the components conceptualized in this framework

2. That contracting is related to pupil growth and assessable (not always measurable in the norm-referenced sense)

3. That teachers are the best determiners of task allocation and its application with students and, therefore, possess the basis for deciding upon subsequent remuneration

4. That if performance contracting is to be a reform, the decision-making structure of educational systems must be radically altered to enable teachers at the grass-roots level not only the accountability, but the capability of mustering resources to accomplish desired ends

Critical Ingredients of the Mesa Model:

1. The derivation of a systematic needs assessment of pupils by which the goals of the school system are stated in performance terms

2. The development of performance objectives at various levels within the schools

3. The establishment of staff-deployment models contingent upon a task analysis of teacher skills necessary to realize specific sets of pupil objectives

4. The provision of role change (the unbreaking of a given role set) when pupil needs change and a new set of objectives must be specified (in Mesa this is called a

"fluid hierarchy" of roles); provision for a change in time and space relationships in the schools

5. The development of a set of conditions by which the professional staff, through its own professional association, develops contracts for pupil performance with its own board of education.

Generic Steps of the Mesa Approach for Performance Contracting: It was expected that the board of education would develop a request for proposal (RFP). The RFP may be general or specific. The board may use consultants at this point to establish the specifications for the submission of proposals from the staff, or the board may invite the staff to write specific performance statements for its goals and then select the ones it deems most suitable (Figure 6).

The various schools would submit "bids" to the board on what they feel it would cost to fulfill the board's specifications. The board may accept some and reject some. It may accept all or reject all or ask for a second round of "bids." The board may wish to negotiate with the staff over particulars. The negotiations would take place through the previously established professional association's deliberations team of the Mesa Education Association. Contained with a bid would be all items pertaining to instruction, including salaries of all personnel in the bid, overhead, materials, and any subcontracting.

The board may add certain incentives for "enrichment" or penalties for not meeting agreed-upon objectives. Important will be the widening of the contracts to include objectives in the affective areas. The rationale, criteria for goal attainment in noncognitive areas, and type of instrumentation to be used will be subject to negotiations. Some areas will not be conducive to norm-referenced or criterion-referenced instruments. Panels or juries may submit testimony as to whether

FIGURE 6

Arizona-Mesa Differentiated-Staffing Consortium—Mission Profile for Project RFP (Request for Proposal), November–January 1970–1971

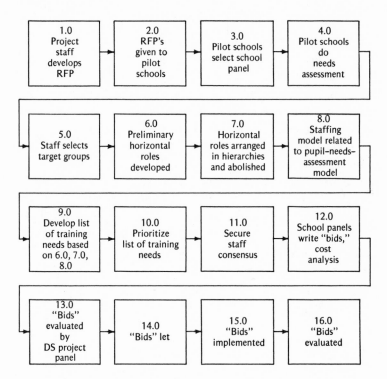

some objectives have been met. Bids will deliberately include objectives in the attitudinal areas subject to educational audits.

High-yielding teaching teams may subcontract with chronic low-yielding teaching teams for their services. High-yielding teams may increase the costs of their bids on the basis of past performance. Middle-management salaries above a base-line salary (principals, supervisors, directors, etc.) may earn a commission as they subcontract their services to teaching teams in the field. This would assure the relevance of central services to the solution of field problems and would force administrative services to remain central to instruction.

The question of remuneration of the team is an issue to be solved by the teaching teams themselves. They may choose to delegate the payment of salaries to an outside agency, the administration, or the teachers' association on the basis of previously specified criteria, or they may directly allocate salaries by an internally agreed-upon mechanism. The board and the administration should remain impartial to the salary mechanism since their first concern is with students and whether the contracting has been met. The granting of direct blocks of cash to teachers may greatly facilitate the development of internal professional standards of performance and assist in the development of an internal mechanism of peer regulation. Since this remains the essence of professionalism, seen in this perspective, teacher governance is stimulated. Further, it is directly related to pupil benefits, something very much absent at the present time.

The essence of the Mesa approach is that performance contracting can become the mechanism by which pupil benefits are established, teacher governance is enhanced, and the restructuring of the school system into a nonlinear system is brought about. That these elements are viewed as ultimately compatible is the hope of the education professions for growth towards full professional status, which derives professional privileges by meeting its professional responsibilities.

Figure 7 shows the steps by which the accountability or contracting system is employed, and differentiated staffing is a means in this process. Then, the actual differentiated-staffing project RFP is shown, by which Mesa teachers at the differentiated staff pilot schools underwent the "bidding" procedures inherent in the Mesa design. It is reproduced here.

FIGURE 7

A Mesa Public Schools Tentative System Model for Internal Educational Performance Contracting

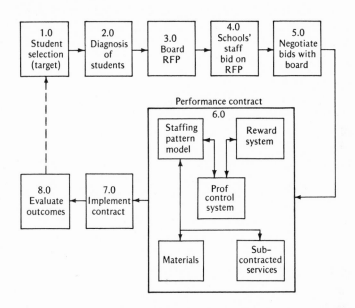

Questions pertaining to procedures, evaluation, arbitration and involvement will be answered by studying it in some detail.

Number	Task
1	Selection of a target group of students
2	Diagnosis of students (a comparison of student performance with validated student base-line objectives)
3	Board of education draws up a request for proposal (RFP) from teaching teams based upon #1 and #2
4	Schools or individual teams within schools may bid on RFP
5	Bids are negotiated through the professional-association deliberations team with board or designate

Number	Task
6	A contract is drawn up incorporating the following: a. Minimum expectancy levels for students b. Cost breakdowns of salaries, overhead, materials, and contracted services with the administration or outside groups (this may include the cost of team in-service training) c. Agreed-upon time limits necessary to reach objectives d. Penalty or other incentives if objectives are exceeded or not reached e. Type of staffing pattern to be deployed and a generic listing of differentiated roles f. Type of reward structure to be followed upon contract completion (what procedures to be followed in distributing pay; internal and external procedures and criteria) g. Type of evaluation and instrumentation to be used
7	Implementation of contact
8	Evaluation of student outcomes
9	Feedback on student performance, regrouping, selection of new targets, diagnosis, drawing up of further RFPs, etc.

ACTUAL COPY OF REQUEST FOR PROPOSAL INSTRUCTION SHEET FOR TEACHERS

Background

The Mesa Differentiated-Staffing Project calls for school staffs to submit "bids" to the board of education to educate their students to achieve specific outcomes.

This request for proposal (RFP) closely parallels what teachers will be deliberating with the Mesa Board of Education later in the spring. However, it is chiefly confined to teacher objectives to attain the goals of the differentiated-staffing project.

Read these instructions as a guide in preparing your "bid" on the project RFP. The RFP spells out what should be in your "bid" to reach the objectives of the project.

Recommended Procedure for Bidding
It is recommended that school staffs follow this procedure in preparing their "bid" on the project RFP.

1. Faculty nominates staff steering committee to perform the task of coordination (can be faculty senates if they have already been elected, or an appointed committee of faculty senates).
2. Faculty staff steering committee performs task of data gathering and writing staff "bid," securing staff consensus and negotiating bid.
3. Faculty staff steering committee performs staff liaison with entire school staff during "bid" implementation and in representing the staff on other formal ongoing deliberations with the project staff such as:
   a. Deliberating ongoing changes in the original objectives should progress indicate objectives are unrealistic or need alteration (see RFP for specification of tolerance limits)
   b. Receiving and presenting staff grievances during the time the staff is functioning under the conditions of the "bid"
   c. Working with the staff as an evaluative body of consultants, project management and direction, and public relations to explain the program to the press and community, set up visitation procedures, and other on-site evaluation procedures by outside persons or agencies
4. Faculty staff steering committees should be elected and serve staggered terms so that a portion of the group is continually replaced, but that enough experience is retained so as not to present an unusually high degree of unsophistication with the process.

5. The entire school staff should set criteria of selection by which teachers are elected to the staff steering committee; MEA (Mesa Education Association) building representatives may have an automatic seat as either a voting member or an exofficio representative of the MEA.

GUIDELINES FOR THE REQUEST FOR PROPOSAL (RFP)

Directions: Guidelines for RFPs are to be used in the preparation of staff "bids" for project resources to meet the following objectives:

1. To complete the pilot school's staffing model with the following components:
   a. A well-defined horizontal level of role specification which contains at least *three* distinctive roles
   b. The illustration of at least three plans by which horizontal roles may form a vertical hierarchy in relationship to one another and are subsequently abolished when specified pupil objectives have been met
   c. A cost-defined training component based upon role specialization and costs of implementation
2. The development of a general needs-assessment model for the total school, utilizing the Kaufman-system approach and from which future bids will be designed and deliberated
3. The clear linkage between the proposal staffing model and the needs assessment model (not the needs assessment itself)

Time Constraints:

Bids are due for evaluation by the project staff by November 27, 1970. The preceding requirements for this RFP to be met by January 22, 1971.

1. This leaves approximately ten working days for "bid" preparation.

2. Bids will be deliberated during the week of November 30–December 4.
3. From the December 4 date, approximately 35 working days are available for staffs to complete their "bid." This includes the feasibility of working during the Christmas holidays for those teachers so desiring.

Bid Preparation:

Bids should follow closely this format suggested in the RFP, and be typed on ditto so that many copies are available for the evaluation panel and subsequent deliberations; 25 copies of the "bid" should be submitted on the deadline date.

Evaluation Panel:

The evaluation panel will consist of the following representatives:

1. Two members of the project staff
2. A member of the central office
3. Two members representing the Mesa Educational Association
4. If desired or necessary, outside consultants

Evaluation Criteria for Bids:

1. To what extent are the "bids" representing project objectives?
2. Are the "bids" feasible, can they be accomplished in the time period designated and with funds requested?
3. What evidence is there for staff involvement and staff consensus?
4. Does the instrumentation for evaluation, or evaluation methods, appear to be reasonable?
5. Are the staffing roles supported by a sound needs-assessment of students? Are they flexible and changeable? How? Under what conditions?

Bid Deliberation:

The project-evaluation panel will meet with the school steering committee to deliberate bids. The school steering committee should be empowered to deal with the project-evaluation panel. Final "bid" acceptance should rest upon staff consensus, that is, the school steering committee represents the staff during deliberations, but final acceptance rests with the staff. Staffs determine the acceptable consensus level to enter into a "bid."

BID FORMAT:

"Bids" should follow the recommended format below and conform to the desired number of pages. Additional information submitted by schools occurs in the attachment of appendices at the end of the "bid." The title page should include: School name, number of personnel and students in bid, and bid title (denoting major areas covered).

Section I—Opening Statement—Bid Abstract (1 page):

A one-page overview of the "bid" which includes (1) major objectives, (2) major activities, and (3) major evaluation activities.

Section II—Bid Budget (1–2 pages):

List as follows: Provide for two columns. In the left-hand side state the objectives of the bid in performance terms. In the right-hand side list the dollar figure which you have calculated necessary to reach the objective. After each figure indicate method of arriving at the figure. For example:

1. 15 teachers at $4 per hour $\times$ 4 hours per day $\times$ 10 days = $2,400.

2. Visitation mileage at 10¢ a mile × 700 miles = $70.

Unipac on Personal Responsibility in Our Society:

1. Will include objectives in all learning domains
2. Provision for three classifications of materials, including enrichment and remediation components
3. Provision for differentiated instruction
   a. Large groups
   b. Discussion groups
   c. Tutorial or independent
4. Pretest and provision for varying entry levels
5. 500 copies (including duplicating cost) = $550.

Section III—Body of Bid (not more than 5 pages)

1. Description of needs-assessment model used to delineate student needs.
2. Method by which student needs are linked to staffing roles (rationale).
3. Show at least two schemata by which roles are changed in response to a hypothetical change in student needs as a result of instruction.
4. List tentative (brief) job descriptions for horizontal roles.
5. Cite any kind of subcontracting proposed in bid.
6. Cite need for intradistrict consultant help.
7. Cite need for any other type of help in meeting bid.
8. Specify the precise time periods of instruction (travel, site observation, research).

Section IV—Training Program (2–3 pages)

1. Identify target group of teachers in program.
2. Identify necessary entry-level skills teachers must have in order to enter training.
3. Relate training needs to skills necessary to meet student objectives.
4. State type and kind of training program desired (cite specific training outcomes desired).
5. Identify any consultants you specifically desire to include in the "bid."

6. Identify sequence and approximate amount of time to be spent on each training activity.
7. Break training objectives into cognitive, affective, and psychomotor domains.

Section V—Evaluation (2–3 pages)

1. Identify how a self-correcting mechanism is capable of making midcourse corrections of the training program as staff needs change.
2. Approximately a 20 percent latitude of change in the original objectives is permitted to be altered as a normal part of adjusting ongoing needs to target objectives; if more is desired, up to 50 percent can be deliberated on an ongoing basis.
3. Type of evaluation procedures to be employed in evaluating outcomes—these may include standardized tests, teacher-made tests, observation, anecdotal data, testimonials, audits, juries; in case juries are proposed, state the type or specific names of those desired on such an evaluation panel.
4. Cite the name of an impartial referee in case of disagreement between outside panel or staff if the jury system is utilized.
5. Approximately 10 percent of the bid should be withheld to be distributed to the staff in terms of bonuses if the contract is met on the time line indicated. If the contract is successfully met, propose the criteria on which the funds would be distributed and the mechanism by which it would happen (i.e., staff distributes funds, administration distributes funds, education association distributes funds). This will be subject to deliberation and must be in harmony with EPDA guidelines.
6. Training objectives should encompass some objectives in the attitudinal areas—cite ways you intend to gather data.

Illustrations: Functional block-flow diagrams illustrating project profile and project functions are appreciated but not mandatory.

SPECIFICATIONS ON THE GRIEVANCE PROCEDURE

The primary purpose of establishing a systematic grievance procedure is to ensure that all are not only able to participate, but that all staff opinions are considered in submitting a "bid." The grievance procedure provides for the filing of a minority report should any staff member or members feel that their opinions, ideas, or feelings in the deliberation process have not been duly considered.

What Is a Grievance?

A grievance is defined broadly as a "circumstance or condition thought to be unjust and ground for complaint or resentment. The injury may be wrong, real, or imagined." Some practical examples are:

1. If there is disagreement by any staff member over any aspect of the school "bid" (conditions, procedures, etc.)
2. A feeling that any particular decision was made without proper involvement

A Grievance Report

A grievance should be in writing and signed. It should cite particular and specific instances if possible.

With Whom Should a Grievance Be Filed?

A written grievance should be filed in the following manner:

1. The grievance should be filed first with the school's own "bid" panel, senate, or steering committee.
2. The grievance may be referred by the school body (senate, steering committee, etc.) to the differentiated-staff project "bid" panel, or by the individual(s) on the school staff, once having heard the course of action decided by the local school body.
3. The grievance should be filed last with the Mesa Education Association's grievance committee if action to the

point of filing has not been satisfactory in the eyes of those presenting the grievance.

RFP MODEL SPECIFICATIONS[3]

Background

In the past, differentiated staffing has meant only the creation of new roles based upon an additive method of model construction. Such a procedure begins by taking the role of classroom teacher and "adding" on more responsibilities, which are then equated with a range of pay. A schema showing this approach is shown below:

THE ADDITIVE METHOD OF
DIFFERENTIATED-STAFFING MODEL BUILDING

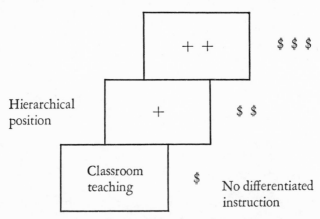

Such models have been dubbed "generation I" models of staff differentiation, that is, they typically begin with the solution to a teacher problem, rather than with a systematic assessment of the needs of children and *differentiating instruction* to meet the needs of children.

[3] To be contained in the body of the "Bid," Section III.

Criteria for the Mesa Model

The Mesa model is really a misnomer. It is rather, a process by which any teaching staff examines in a systematic way what they must do to meet the requirements of a relevant educational program for their students. Criteria for the Mesa Model are as follows:

1. Staffing roles and patterns must be concretely related via needs assessment by pupils.
2. Staffing patterns must have the capacity for flexible deployment and position as student needs change with instruction.
3. Hierarchical position of a role is related to the need for *differentiated instruction* (ID and DS), and skills of the teacher are grouped on that basis, instead of merely adding onto or subtracting from the current definition of classroom-teaching responsibilities.

SOME SUGGESTED FOCI FOR
DIFFERENTIATING INSTRUCTION

How can instruction be differentiated and related to staff differentiation? There are a number of ways of looking at learning and the teacher's responsibilities held by educators such as Robert M. Gagne.

Teaching Functions Which
Could Be Differentiated and Regrouped

Teaching functions have been broadly classified as these six:

1. Learning objectives (writing objectives)
2. Decisions concerning the nature of knowledge to be learned (curriculum)
3. Motivation
4. Arranging the conditions appropriate for learning to occur (learning environment)

5. Arranging for transferability of what is learned
6. Assessment (evaluation)

One method of differentiating instruction is to have some teachers specializing in various substeps listed earlier. For example, some teachers could specialize in the arrangement of learning conditions and consult with other teachers on how to improve the conditions of learning. Another could specialize on assessment. All are directly working with children. All may perform each subfunction, but some may specialize in particular substeps. Another type of differentiated instruction which could be considered is the modes of instruction. These refer to the pattern of methodology employed by the teacher. These may be

1. Tutoring (one to one)
2. Lecturing (large group)
3. Reciting
4. Group discussion (seminar)
5. The laboratory
6. Inquiry methods
7. Curriculum packets
8. Using technological aides

Differentiated roles should emanate directly from efforts at differentiating instruction, because pupils should be differentiated. Changing staffing roles without visible links to pupil needs may not improve instruction at all.

What Is a Complete Model?
A complete model would be one in which the staff had selected a number of possible combinations from the preceding list or others and used them to differentiate instruction. A ranking of roles, or the establishment of a hierarchy, should depend largely on the conditions of the "bid"; that is, roles should assume a natural ranking once student needs are

assessed and specific objectives established with the board of education.

What the staff presents in *this* "bid" should reflect their thinking regarding how objectives might be realized, and should anticipate their training needs accordingly.

Bid Monitoring

The evaluation panel and project staff will perform ongoing monitoring once "bids" have been let. In addition, it is understood that the evaluation panel may request interim reports as needed or desired. If other parties are to function in a "monitoring" capacity, they should be designated in the original bid and accepted in the deliberation process. If an interim report should indicate that faulty progress is being made, the evaluation panel is empowered to make suggestions which must be carried out by the school staff. The school staff may dispute the finding or conclusion of the evaluation panel, asking for a referral to the arbitrator. The arbitrator must file a report within two days from the time of referral. If the arbitrator agrees, the school staff must comply. If he does not, the "bid" continues without alteration.

Arbitration of Results

Since "bid" objectives will be stated in performance terms, there is a built-in evaluation strategy. However, upon completion of the bid, the evaluation panel may challenge the data of the bid completion in the final report. In order to anticipate such possibilities, an outside "arbitrator" should be designated and accepted for deliberations. "Bids" should contain the names of several possible arbitrators when submitted.

If the final report is disputed by the evaluation panel, the designated arbitrators' decision is final. Arbitrators have ten days to file a report if the bid-completion data is challenged.

Final Report

Upon completion of the "bid," the school staff is expected to file a final report. The final report should follow this format.

Section I—1-page summary: A one-page summary of what was attempted and what the results were.

Section II—evidence of bid completion: What is presented in this section is evidence (factual, statistical, and anecdotal) of bid completion.

Section III—review and recommendations: The staff offers a written review of progress and makes recommendations it feels should be considered in the next RFP.

Section IV—financial audit: An accounting of where money was spent may be necessary if expenditures are challenged. The final report should not be longer than 20–25 pages with whatever appendices are necessary to document the completion of the "bid."

chapter
three

Planning and Implementing an FIO Model

Many advocates of change have suggested that the only way to change education and educational practices is through the implementation of massive change rather than through numerous small changes. The rationale behind this position is that it is easier to adjust to massive change than to a series of minor changes. People are constantly kept off balance when they are required to make a long series of adjustments. A collateral hypothesis might be that it is less nerve-wracking to contract pneumonia and have it cured than to suffer through a succession of lingering colds. This hypothesis may be questioned, but the contention that the implementation of a flexible instructional organization requires massive change is indisputable. The experience of school districts with FIO, as seen in the previous chapter and the models, leaves little doubt that extensive change is a concomitant of a flexible instructional organization.

Experience has proven that, due to changes required, the planning of an FIO model is not a task to be taken lightly. The lighthouse school districts across the country, including those found preceding this chapter, have devoted extensive time and effort to planning their models. The problem of planning an FIO model is further complicated by the maxim that there is no "best" way to do anything in education, because we are dealing with the individual and unstable differences found in students, teachers, communities, and resources. Therefore, an FIO model designed for one school district would probably not be the best model for another school district. The suggestion is not being made that every model must be unique. There may be common elements, but each school district must provide, through adaptation, for its own uniqueness. It follows then, that each school district must plan its own FIO model. Due to the complexity of an FIO model, there is need for a rational, systematic approach to planning. Effective planning has been called the first step to successful implementation, but implementation also requires specific planning. The discussion in this chapter, will center on the principles and procedures involved in planning and implementing an FIO model. In addition, a suggested planning and implementation schedule will be included.

THE PLANNING PROCESS

All people, consciously or unconsciously, engage in some type of planning process; in some cases, rather primitive and in others, rather sophisticated. Compared to other fields of endeavor, educators as a group must be considered comparatively unsophisticated planners. This is not meant as an indictment of educators, because there is little in our background that prepares us to engage in anything but the most superficial types of planning. On the contrary, educators must be commended for the progress they have made despite the limited preparation for planning that they have received.

Traditional Planning Process

The first step in any planning process is to identify a problem that needs solution. In education we have often started with the task of deciding on which of two solutions should be selected to solve an unstated problem rather than a true problem. An example of this procedure is a school district which is attempting to decide whether to hire a remedial-reading teacher or purchase a programmed remedial-reading series. Actually, neither of these solutions may be appropriate for the type of reading problems that trouble the children in that school district. Whether the process is started with true problems or alternative solutions, the fact remains that a solution must be found or a decision made. Typically, a solution of some kind is generated and examined to determine which of the subproblems it will solve. If the planners are impressed with the solution, they decide to use it. If not, they continue their search until they are suitably impressed with a solution and adopt it. In some cases, perfunctory plans concerning implementation procedures are prepared prior to adoption, but more often than not, implementation is planned as the solution is being implemented. Since the solution is often not completely suitable and implementation has been superficial, it begins to irritate everyone associated with it; but, somehow, people learn to live with minor irritants. They continue to live with this aggravation until it becomes unbearable. At this point the planning cycle starts again, and eventually, the laws of probability dictate that the correct solution will be found.

In 1901, John Dewey gave the following account of this type of planning and educational change:

Consider the way by which a new study is introduced into the curriculum. Someone feels that the school system of his . . .

town is falling behind the times. There are rumors of great progress in education being made elsewhere. Something new and important has been introduced; education is being revolutionized by it; the superintendent and board become somewhat uneasy; the matter is taken up by individuals and clubs; pressure is brought to bear on the school system; letters are written to the newspapers . . . editorials appear; finally the school board ordains that on and after a certain date the particular new brand . . . shall be taught in the public schools. The victory is won, and everybody—unless it be some already overburdened and distracted teachers—congratulates everybody else that such advanced steps are taken.[1]

If Dewey was satirizing this type of planning in 1901 when life was relatively simple, what might he be saying today when life and the educational process have become so complex? A rational view of the traditional planning process would dictate the conclusion that it is no longer viable, if for no other reason than that it is too expensive today to make mistakes in planning. Fortunately, planners in other professions have devised an assortment of planning models for use in a variety of situations, so there is no need for educators to develop their own planning models. Of the many models they have devised, the systems model appears to have the most potential for providing educators with the conceptual planning tools that they need.

Systems Planning

Systems planning or the systems approach to planning has been traced back to the British military use of "operations research" to adapt radar to military use during the early thirties. In this country, the Department of Defense has demonstrated its potential and popularized its use. Today, few organizations, NASA among others, have not utilized the

[1] John Dewey, NEA *Proceedings,* 1901, pp. 334–335.

systems approach to planning in one form or another. The now familiar planning-programming-budgeting-system (PPBS) is one form of the systems approach. The model offered here should not be considered a formula which must be adhered to at all costs. Steps may be added or combined as necessary to suit local needs, but the basic intent and general sequence should be retained. The steps presented here will be discussed in relation to planning an FIO model. The steps are:

1. Identify the correct problem
2. Decide on performance requirements
3. Determine constraints
4. Perform gross functional analysis
5. State alternatives
6. Select best alternatives
7. Determine planning priorities
8. Develop a planning schedule
9. Define mission objectives for each functional component
10. List and analyze vital functions
11. List performance tasks
12. Suggest alternative methods and means
13. Select best alternatives
14. Assemble components—iteration
15. Perform design trade-off
16. Define performance specifications
17. Test and evaluate
18. Modify as needed

Step 1: Identify the correct problem. Under normal conditions this is not always an easy task, but for our purposes it is relatively easy. The problem is to develop a flexible instructional-organizational model.

Step 2: Decide on performance requirements. decide on what the FIO model should be able to accomplish. In educational terms, this step requires a statement of the objectives for the FIO model. At this stage in the planning process, they would be general or overall objectives. These objectives will be discussed later in the process.

Step 3: Determine constraints. Constraints are any factors or conditions that will impose limitations on the solutions being considered. For an FIO model, this would include budgetary restraints; physical facilities available; state laws governing personnel, curriculum, hours of instruction, budget, and certification; community resources; community sentiment; expertise of current staff-members; pressure groups; and the nature of the learner. Clearly, this is not a definitive list of possible constraints which might limit decision making. If there is such a thing as a crucial step in the planning process, this step would be it. The constraints identified become pivotal points on which all future decisions are weighed. It would be most disheartening to discover that a particularly innovative instructional schedule which had required countless hours of planning was in violation of a state law. If the planners of the instructional schedule are aware of the state law, they can either attempt to work within the constraints of the law or receive a dispensation in the name of experimentation from the state department of education. As can be seen in this example, an explication of the constraints operative in a particular situation can save many false starts and the discarding of excellent but inappropriate solutions. There is no substitute for knowing precisely the limits within which decisions can or must be made.

Step 4: Performing gross functional analysis. Gross functional analysis requires that the overall objectives, stated earlier, be analyzed to determine the types of functions which must be performed to achieve the objectives. For a flexible instructional-organization model, the functions would probably include curriculum, instruction, personnel, utilization of facilities, decision making, administrative organization, and instructional scheduling. The categories listed here tend to be traditional, but at the next step in the process these categories could change.

Step 5: State alternatives. The process used at this step could be called brainstorming. The functions identified in step 4 are used to generate as many categories as possible. The purpose here is to be sure that no function, no matter how remotely related, will be overlooked.

This appears to be an excellent time to point out a distinguishing characteristic of the systems approach to planning. The process described for both this step and step 3 require that a particular universe be examined carefully to identify any factors or conditions which may affect the process or the decisions to be made. This process can be conceptualized as a radar device that is constantly scanning the environment looking for the enemy. The enemy of any planning project is an unknown factor that could disrupt the planning process or destroy the final plans. Hence, the constant search for potential troublemakers. The familiar quotation about "the best laid plans of mice and men" applies here. Even the most effectively planned projects are victims of unexpected problems. The motto of any planning group might be: "Why add avoidable burdens when the unavoidable or unknown will create more than enough problems?"

Step 6: Select best alternatives. The many alternatives generated at step 5 are now examined to determine the functions that will contribute most to efficient planning. Combining, restating, and refining may be required before the best alternatives can be selected. The significance of this step can be seen in the fact that the functions selected here become the missions for the task forces that will engage in planning for each function. For example, if three of the selected functions are the roles and responsibilities of professional and paraprofessional instructional personnel, curriculum, and instruction, then task forces will be assigned the responsibility of preparing the plans needed for each of these areas. What started as traditional categories at step 4 may have evolved, by creative thinking, into unorthodox but extremely useful categories.

Step 7: Determine planning priorities. In systems language, this step might be referred to as *queuing,* which in the vernacular means waiting line. This term refers to the process of determining the priorities for each task to be performed and lining them in the order in which they must be accomplished. Successful queuing can be accomplished if two factors are taken into account. First, each function or component of the FIO model must be analyzed to determine if the results of the planning for that component are prerequisites for the planning of another component. Conversely, each component must be analyzed to determine if other components must be planned before it can be planned. An example may clarify this process. If the component under consideration is the instructional program, it would normally be considered a prerequisite to planning a scheduling system. Clearly, it would be difficult to prepare a system for scheduling classes until something was known about the instructional program. On the other hand, a group attempting to plan an instructional program would be hampered unless they had some knowledge of the curriculum. Therefore, the curriculum becomes a prerequisite for the instructional program.

Second, an estimation must be made of the time required to plan each component. However, when time estimates are being made, consideration must include the possibility that planning may start for one component before the planning is completed for a prerequisite component. For example, the group responsible for planning a scheduling system may start searching for systems used by other school districts before the plans for the instructional program are completed.

Step 8: Develop a planning schedule.   When the time and sequence decisions are made for each component as specified in step 7, a planning schedule can be prepared to graphically illustrate the starting and ending times for the planning of each component. The process described in step 6 and here may suggest that a PERT (program evaluation and review technique) chart is being suggested. In some respects this is true, but the planning schedule being recommended here does not require the precise calculations called for in developing a PERT chart. The graphic illustration of the planning schedule may take the form of either Figures 4 or 5 in model C, with starting date and explanatory text included. The purpose of the planning schedule is to guide staff members involved in the planning process and to apprise other interested parties of the activities of the planning staff.

Step 9: Define mission objectives for each functional component.   Following the preparation of the planning schedule, each functional component is analyzed to ascertain, by the task force assigned to do the planning, the mission objectives—that is, the objectives that the planners expect to achieve as they plan for the component. Included in this process would be a definition of the performance requirements for the component similar to the process described in step 2.

Step 10: List and analyze vital functions.   The tasks to be performed at this step are similar to those described in step 4, where gross functions were identified. The difference here is that all the specific functions must be identified. The functions identified at this stage in the planning process will be used to prepare the detailed and explicit plans for each component which will later be implemented. Obviously, the identification of functions must be performed with great diligence and care. In the planning of curriculum, the functions identified at this step in the process serve as a basis for determining the types of content, including skills, that will be included in the curriculum.

Before the next step is discussed, a reminder must be included here. As each task force proceeds with its planning for the functional component that is its responsibility, the constraints identified at step 3 must constantly be reviewed. This is to guarantee that the plans being made will conform to the limits imposed by the constraints. A principle of the systems approach to planning is that every decision must be filtered through the known constraints.

Step 11: List performance tasks. The performance tasks can be identified by asking, "What tasks must be performed to insure that the functions stated at step 10 will be accomplished?" One of the functions identified at step 10 might be the ability to utilize library resources. The tasks necessary to fulfill this function might include the ability to use a card catalog, knowledge of how to locate nonfiction books, familiarity with major reference works, and so on.

Step 12: Suggest alternative methods and means. This step calls for another brainstorming session. Since, as was suggested earlier, there is no best way to do anything in education, the obvious conclusion is that there are many possible ways to accomplish a specific task. Therefore, at this step, the task force must generate many methods for accomplishing each of the tasks. Contrary to the opinions of many foes of the systems approach, this type of activity, required in the systems approach, has the potential of producing more creative solutions for the problems facing educators than the traditional approach to planning. Many critics of the systems approach claim that it is too rigid and stifling, but as seen here, this criticism has little foundation in fact.

Step 13: Select the best alternative. For the second time, the process calls for an examination of all the alternatives to determine which methods or means will be adopted. There appear to be at least four, and perhaps more, criteria that can be used as guides for making these decisions. The planners should feel free to add criteria if it will assist them in selecting the best alternatives. The first criterion would be the constraints identified earlier or new constraints that have come to the attention of the planners. Second, the effectiveness of each alternative should be pinpointed, if possible. Unfortunately, this is a very difficult procedure in education. The data needed to determine whether a particular product or procedure is more effective than any other is not often available. Recognizing this limitation, the decision-makers must obtain whatever data is available, no matter how insignificant it may seem, and use it in reaching a decision. Granted, this is not a very exacting approach, but it is preferable to selecting a product because it is attractively packaged. As time goes by and educators begin requesting data, the producers of educational products and the advocates of particular procedures will begin providing significant data.

Third, the efficiency of each alternative should be determined. What is needed here is the computing of a cost-effectiveness ratio for each alternative. A cost-effectiveness ratio will indicate the degree of effectiveness that can be expected for each dollar or unit of expenditure required by each alternative. Again, in education this is a difficult procedure, but as suggested earlier, making a decision based on limited data is better than making a decision on no data. Fourth, the last and conceivably most critical criterion is the needs of the people who will serve or be served by the system. Actually, this fourth criterion might well be one of the constraints, but because of its strategic importance it is being singled out here to establish its significance. A cardinal rule for planners of a flexible instructional organization might be that the model must be designed to accommodate the students and staff rather than force them to adjust to the FIO model. Since people differ, some adjustment on their part may be unavoidable, but every effort must be made to keep involuntary compliance with the model at a minimum. Consequently, each alternative must be analyzed to insure that the needs of students and staff are not compromised.

Step 14: Assemble components. As the decisions for each element of the functional components are made, the process of assembling the components can begin. In systems terminology, this process is called *iteration.* The process calls for continuous and repeated evaluation of each step with prior analysis steps and stated mission objectives to insure that the final product will conform to the stated performance requirements (step 2) and satisfy mission objectives (step 9). The objective of system iteration techniques is compatibility between the functions to be performed by each component and organizational requirements in achieving stated objectives. Although it was not called iteration, the implication was there when it was recommended that each decision should be checked against objectives and filtered through the system constraints. By using the objectives and constraints as reference points, the planners can feel secure that they will not drift off course. The same process would be used as the components are assembled to produce a total flexible instructional organization.

Step 15: Perform design trade-off. As components of the total FIO model are being assembled, the data generated at step 13 are used to perform *design trade-off.* Trade-off involves the weighing of the alternative means and components for achieving the stated objectives, for the purpose of selecting the one that is the most economical and still is capable of achieving the objectives. The trade-off is between economy and effectiveness, taking into consideration that more cannot be spent than is available, but also that the objectives cannot be compromised for economic reasons. Although this may be a very wrenching experience for the planners of each of the components, it can be doubly so for those responsible for assembling the total FIO model if the component planners have exceeded their fiscal constraints. The only counsel that can be given to planners involved in the trade-off process is that they should be prepared to devote considerable time to completing the process.

Step 16: Define performance specifications. The definition of performance specifications in educational terms means specifying evaluative criteria and techniques. Chapter 5 is devoted to a detailed discussion of the procedures to be used at this step, so no explanation will be presented here.

Step 17: Test and evaluate model. Step 17 occurs after the system, in this case the FIO model, has been implemented. This step is also discussed in detail in Chapter 5.

Step 18: Modify model as needed. As a result of the testing and evaluation of the implemented FIO model, certain dysfunctions or problems will appear. The data concerning the dysfunctions are analyzed to determine the possible causes and are used to modify the system. The data concerning dysfunctions is called feedback and will be discussed in the next chapter.

PREPARING FOR IMPLEMENTATION

Successful implementation, as has been stated, will depend on effective planning of the FIO model, but more important, the willingness and ability of the school staff to change will be the determining factor. Any school organization has the potential of helping or hindering the instructional program; however, no organization can compensate for reluctant or inadequately prepared people. Consequently, any plan for implementation must take into account the human factor, but educating people so that they can accept a new organization and method of operating is not easily accomplished. Lippitt points out:

> Learning the new educational practice, therefore, is not a simple matter of absorbing the written transmission of information. An active learning process involving various "levels" of the person is required. To make this change requires more commitment, risk taking, and help from others than is true in the other field of practice. Consequently, more apathy or resistance can be expected, and more support is needed from peers and supervisors. Further, more guidance is needed from consultants, trainers, demonstrators; and experimental opportunities are essential in the school setting.[2]

Without question, then, provisions must be made to assist staff members to make the adjustments necessary for successful implementation of a flexible instructional organization.

Preparing for Change

A flexible instructional organization will require staff members to accept changes in their working relationships with other staff members and with students in curriculum, instructional strategies, instructional modes, and instructional schedules. To assist staff members in adjusting to these changes, some thought should be given to conditions that may maximize their ability and desire to change.

People must see a need for change before they will accept a change. The mistake should not be made of assuming that simply pointing out the disadvantages of the existing system and the advantages of the new system will convince teachers that a change is needed. The implication of this strategy is that everything the teachers and administrators have been doing, in some cases for years, has been wrong. Even if this

---

[2] Ronald Lippitt *et al.,* "The Teachers as Innovator, Seeker, and Sharer of New Practices," in *Prospectives on Educational Change,* ed. Richard I. Miller, New York: Appleton, 1967, p. 308.

is true, many teachers and administrators resent admitting it to themselves, let alone making a public confession. Care must be taken to avoid condemning past practices. If the staff is exposed to the advantage of the new flexible instructional organization, they may accept the need for a change, particularly if they are not subjected to high-pressure tactics. In an FIO project, it is not necessary to have all staff members accept the change, because for the first few years the dissenters need not be involved in the change.

To accept change, people must understand the implications of the change. Everyone has had the experience of watching a proponent of change face a barrage of questions which begin with, "What will happen to . . . ?" Part of the fear associated with anything new is rooted in the effect that the proposed change may have on the countless relationships, ways of working, behaviors, activities, and so on, that make up life and work. People can rationalize and accept substantial confusion and inconvenience associated with present conditions. They know what they have, both good and bad, and are not eager to accept an unknown quality. The old adage, "A bird in the hand is worth two in the bush," reflects the attitude of many people. This anxiety about the unknown can be overcome to some degree by anticipating the "What will happen to . . ." questions and having the answers available. Further, an open climate must be maintained. This means no hidden agenda and a willingness to answer any questions.

To accept change people must feel secure. Security comes from several sources. First, people must have the knowledges and skills necessary to function in a new situation. Unless they have these no real change will occur. An excellent example of what can happen when teachers are not properly prepared for a change is the move to modern math. Many teachers were given short cram courses dealing with the what and how of teaching modern math. They obviously did not acquire the knowledge and skill necessary to teach it, because they reverted to teaching the old arithmetic using modern math books.

Next, people need support from others to accept the change. The example preceding is indicative of how people behave when support is not provided. Teachers may agree to adopt a new program but will not necessarily accept it. Therefore, they must receive support from their peers and supervisory personnel. The needed support may take the form of recognition that no one is expected to be totally effective with the new procedure or organization, acceptance of mistakes, and help in solving problems when they arise. Lastly, people need time to change. Many of the plans designed to implement a modern math program ignored this principle and, in effect, insured failure. A related principle was also operative in the modern math adoption plans. Before people can learn a new procedure or concept, they must unlearn the procedures or concepts they know. Further, the longer they have used the procedures or concepts; the more difficult they are to unlearn. Consequently, it would be expected that the new teachers can change more readily than more experienced teachers. In any case, time must be available for people to change.

Guidelines for Implementation
Planning for implementation should begin when the decision is made to consider the possible adoption of a flexible instructional organization and continue through the planning stages. As has been emphasized, successful implementation will depend on people, not the FIO model. Flaws in the FIO model will be relatively easy to correct compared to fractures in the attitudes, feelings, and emotions of the staff caused by ill-prepared plans to assist them in changing. The discussion here will, therefore, center on conditions that will enhance the planning of the FIO model and, especially, the ultimate implementation of the model.

The first step to be taken is to seek a staff consensus that the possibility of developing an FIO model should be investigated. Representatives of the teachers' bargaining agent, if one exists, should be involved at this stage and all subsequent stages. Exclusion will almost guarantee opposition. A useful technique is to involve the staff in some form of inservice education to provide them with information to allow them to make an intelligent and, hopefully, reasoned decision. At the conclusion of the dissemination sessions, the first "go-no go" decision point is reached. A decision that investigation and planning should commence should not require majority vote. As long as the staffs of one or more schools are interested in participating and a consensus of the remaining staff members is to allow the project to continue on an experimental basis, project planning may begin in earnest.

The assumption is being made that the board of education has authorized the project. Related to board approval is community support. A community education program should be part of any FIO project. Although the same commitment is not needed from the community as from the staff, the comprehensive change associated with a flexible instructional organization would require community support, if not participation. The amount of community involvement and degree of education needed will depend on the nature of the community. A wise educator knows his community and never underestimates its power to promote or obstruct.

A project that can potentially affect every segment of the school system requires a group to manage the planning that an FIO model will require. The lighthouse school districts, including those discussed in the models, all formed steering committees to oversee their projects. Each was careful to include members representing the various groups and areas of the school district, especially a representative of the teachers' bargaining agent. They also appointed a full-time project director to serve as an executive secretary for the steering committee and project. Although there may be little evidence to support this position, much of the success of these projects can be traced to the project director. Committees serve very useful functions, but a serious flaw in the workings of a committee is their seeming inability to follow through on the myriad details associated with any task. A full-time project director should be able to provide the needed follow-through and a total view of the project. The cost of retaining a full-time project director may cause some school districts to rationalize the use of the superintendent as project director. Although many reasons can be given for not using the superintendent, the primary reason is that he is already overburdened.

No steering committee would be in a position to engage in all the planning required in an FIO model. Their fundamental functions are to devise the overall planning strategies, determine planning policy, appoint and guide planning groups or task forces, coordinate the work of the task forces, and assemble and approve the final model. The major portion of the planning is carried on by the task forces, which might include task forces to plan curriculum revision, instructional strategies, flexible-scheduling system, evaluation program, in-service education, policies and procedures, roles in the instructional hierarchy, and communication strategies. The task force responsible for communication strategies deserves a few words of explanation. Large planning projects produce masses of information which must be not only organized but also transmitted internally and externally. The internal communication between working groups can normally be handled through the steering committee or project director. External communication with staff not involved in planning and members of the community requires various strategies and means. If these are lacking, the major form of communication will be rumors, which are usually incorrect and can be damaging. Consequently, a task force to handle external communication would serve a useful function which, among other things, may scotch rumors and gain support for the project.

Staffing each of the task forces must be given serious thought. The criteria for selecting participants should be expertise, willingness, and ability to work with others. Staff members should not be appointed to serve on a task force because they are considered below par and might profit from the experience. The other type of staff member to be avoided is the "nit-picking," argumentative, and incompatible individual who may have a contribution to make but is more destructive than constructive. For some reason this type of person seems to volunteer for every committee assignment. Deliberate thought must be given before a decision is made to include such a person on a task force.

Those staff members not being utilized in the planning process should be provided a means for having input into the process. Accusations of not listening cannot be avoided, but regardless, procedures must be available for any interested parties to communicate with the steering committee. The obvious reason is to avoid anxiety. Here are some suggestions, taken from the experience of the funded FIO projects, which should reduce anxiety:

1. Prepare clear and explicit definitions of the roles, functions, and tasks for each position on the instructional hierarchy.
2. Prepare clear and explicit statements of policies and procedures governing hiring, promotion, tenure, and evaluation.
3. Provide a "grandfather" clause to protect tenured teachers.
4. Allow teachers to transfer out of experimental or pilot schools.
5. Provide planners with the resources needed to work productively. This would include released time, if possible, clerical help, space, materials, and consultant help.
6. Provide in-service education for all staff members who

will work in the experimental or pilot schools prior to implementation.

7. Take time to plan properly and in the process provide time for reeducation and acclimatization of the staff.

PLANNING AND IMPLEMENTATION SCHEDULE

The planning and implementation schedule that follows is purely suggestive. The usual admonition that each school district must prepare its own planning and implementation schedule is being included here out of fear that this schedule will be considered mandatory or the schedule will be used to save time. The suggestions made here and elsewhere are what "might be" rather than what "should be." The suggested time schedule for total implementation, for example, may be shortened for small school districts and extended for large school districts. Further, it must be recognized that the suggested activities are gross descriptions of a series of events which should occur at a given step. A procedure for preparing a planning and implementation schedule might be to synthesize the material presented in this chapter and the procedures used by the school districts as described in the models. As a result of this analysis, it should be a relatively simple matter to decide on a schedule that will satisfy the needs of most school districts.

First Year
1. Conduct in-service education for administrative and instructional personnel
2. Conduct awareness campaign for the community
3. Form steering committee and start planning
   a. Define performance requirements—overall objectives
   b. Identify major constraints
   c. Perform gross functional analysis
   d. Develop planning schedule

    e. Define mission objectives for each functional component—task forces

4. Appoint task forces
    a. Communications
    b. Evaluation
    c. Curriculum
    d. Teacher-task analysis—staffing model
    e. Instruction
    f. Others as needed

5. Start work toward accomplishing planning objectives using systems approach described above
    a. Determine educational needs
    b. Define objectives—K–12
    c. Revise curriculum and instructional strategies
    d. Define instructional functions and tasks needed for revised curriculum and instructional strategies—staffing model
    e. Plan flexible scheduling system
    f. Plan evaluation model
    g. Determine types of facilities needed for new program and remodeling necessary
    h. Determine in-service education needs of staff for effective implementation

Second Year
1. Complete curriculum revision
2. Complete staffing model
3. Prepare manual of policies and procedures
    a. Define roles and responsibilities of instructional staff
    b. Policies and procedures regarding selection, promotion, tenure, salary, and evaluation of staff
4. Complete evaluation model and collect bench-mark data
5. Complete flexible-scheduling plan
6. Select pilot school(s)
7. Select staff for school(s)
8. Begin in-service education of staff

9. Complete any needed building alterations
10. Conduct seminars for parents of children in pilot school(s)

Third Year
1. Implement FIO model in pilot school
2. Select phase-two school(s) for implementation
3. Plan FIO model for phase-two school(s)
4. Evaluate FIO model in pilot school(s)
5. Identify problem areas for teachers in pilot school(s)
6. Conduct in-service education program for teachers in pilot school(s) to solve problems identified
7. Revise original in-service program to overcome problems identified in pilot school(s)
8. Conduct in-service education program for phase-two teachers

Fourth Year
1. Implement FIO model in phase-two school(s)
2. Modify, as needed, FIO model in pilot school(s)
3. Collect data and evaluate FIO models in both pilot and phase-two schools
4. Modify curriculum as needed
5. Revise manual of policies and procedures as needed
6. Select phase-three schools
7. Plan FIO model for phase-three schools
8. Revise in-service education programs as needed
9. Conduct in-service education program for both new and experienced teachers as needed

Fifth Year
1. Implement FIO models in phase three schools
2. Make necessary modifications of implemented FIO models
3. Continue collection of data and evaluate previous years' work
4. Revise curriculum, flexible scheduling, policies and pro-

cedures, staffing model, and in-service education programs
as needed
5. Plan FIO models for remaining schools
6. Conduct in-service education for both new and experienced
teachers as needed

Sixth Year
1. Implement FIO models in remaining schools
2. Continue evaluating and refining all dimensions of FIO
model yearly
3. Continue in-service education program as long as necessary

SUMMARY

The planning and implementation of a flexible instructional
organization model has been the focus of this chapter. Examples of both the traditional and the systems approach to
planning were provided. The traditional planning process
was characterized as being primarily based on emotional
judgments. The systems approach to planning was presented
as an 18-step process:

1. Identify the correct problem
2. Decide on performance requirements—overall objectives
3. Determine constraints
4. Perform gross functional analysis
5. State alternatives
6. Select best alternatives
7. Determine planning priorities
8. Develop a planning schedule
9. Define mission objectives for each functional component
10. List and analyze vital functions
11. List performance tasks
12. Suggest alternative methods and means
13. Select best alternatives

14. Assemble components—iteration
15. Perform design trade-off
16. Define performance specifications
17. Test and evaluate model
18. Modify model as needed

Particular emphasis was given to the fact that the willingness and ability of the school staff will be a determining factor in the ultimate success of any FIO model. Therefore, the need to educate the staff so that they can accept change was stressed. Conditions that may contribute to assisting the staff to accept change include:

1. People must see a need for change before they can accept a change
2. To accept change people must understand the implications of the change
3. To accept change people must feel secure:
   a. Have necessary knowledge and skills
   b. Have support of peers and supervisory personnel
   c. Have time to accept change

Guidelines for implementing an FIO model were discussed. They included:

1. Seek staff consensus.
2. Seek community support.
3. Appoint a steering committee.
4. Provide a full-time project director.
5. Form task forces to assist in planning.
6. Assign one task force the responsibility of providing information to staff not involved in the project and to the community.
7. Provide procedures for interested parties to communicate with steering committee.

Finally, a 6-year planning and implementation schedule was provided.

SELECTED BIBLIOGRAPHY

Banathy, Bela H. *Instructional Systems.* Palo Alto, Calif.: Fearon Publishers (1968).

Banghart, Frank W. *Educational Systems Analysis.* New York: Macmillan (1969).

Bennis, Warren G., Kenneth D. Benne and Robert Chin, eds. *The Planning of Change.* New York: Holt, Rinehart & Winston (1961).

Campbell, James H. and Hal W. Hepler, eds. *Decisions in Communication.* Belmont, Calif.: Wadsworth Publishing Company (1965).

Churchman, C. West. *The Systems Approach.* New York: Dell, (1968).

Evarts, Harry F., *Introduction to PERT.* Boston: Allyn & Bacon (1964).

Loughary, John W., *et. al. Man-Machine Systems in Education.* New York: Harper & Row (1966).

Miller, Richard I., ed. *Perspectives on Educational Change.* New York: Appleton (1967).

Project
Management

The planning of an FIO model can become an almost unmanageable project because of its potential size and scope. As indicated in the last chapter, one of the essential tasks of the steering committee is to manage the planning process of the project. The management of any organization, including an ad hoc organization such as the steering committee, requires control, communication, and decision-making procedures. Control, in this context, means the integrating and coordinating of the decision-making process, which is accomplished by screening, routing, scheduling, assigning, coordinating, expediting, and following up the organizational problems. Communication refers to the process of having the correct information in the appropriate place at the appropriate time so that the best possible decisions can be made. The decision-making procedures refer to the systematic procedures to be used by the organization.

This chapter, therefore, will be devoted to providing methods and procedures which may assist the steering committee in performing its managerial functions. This will be accomplished by proposing that the project be conceptualized as a system, providing a systems approach to management, and proposing a systematic decision-making system.

SYSTEMS APPROACH TO MANAGEMENT

Prior to discussing a systems management model, some thought must be given to the nature of a system. For this, a look at *general systems theory* would be most fruitful. General systems theory attempts to define the nature of a system and how it functions. Rather than going into a long discourse on the development of general systems theory, suffice it to say that it has drawn heavily from the biological sciences. Therefore, the human body will be used as an example of a generalized system. A useful definition for a system is that it is a set of components or parts organized in such a way to constrain or guide action toward the accomplishment of the purposes for which it exists. Using the body as an example, it could be said that its primary purpose is to maintain life. To accomplish this purpose, the body has several subsystems which are constrained to function in a particular manner, for example, the digestive system, the circulatory system, the nervous system, and so on.

What Is a System?

All living systems have certain characteristics, which include:

1. A process or processes
2. Input and output
3. A decider
4. An input analyzer
5. A monitoring device

In the human body the primary process consists of combining air, water, and food to maintain life. The input includes the air, water, and food; and the output is energy or life. The decider of a system is that component which guides or directs the process or processes of the system. In the human body, the nervous system is the dominant decider. The input analyzer consists of components which constantly monitor all input that may affect the system. The monitoring device screens all output in search of dysfunctions within the system and maintains a constant check on the state of the system. An example of the operation of the *decider,* the *input analyzer,* and the *monitoring device* is the maintenance of correct body temperature. The body receives food, air, and water as input, and processes it to produce the heat necessary to maintain a body temperature of 98.6 degrees. In addition to food, air, and water, an input for the body is the heat or absence of heat in the environment. All input is analyzed by the various senses to determine external temperatures. As temperatures go up, this information is transmitted to a *decider,* which opens the pores and releases perspiration that cools the body as it evaporates. A monitoring device maintains a constant check on body temperature. As the body temperature rises, the monitoring device keeps the decider constantly apprised of the need for dropping body temperature. The decider keeps increasing the flow of perspiration to keep the body temperature within tolerable limits. Should the person insist on engaging in strenuous activity despite the heat, the decider will bring the activity to a halt by inducing unconsciousness. The opposite occurs if the external temperature causes the body to cool. Pores close, and more fuel is burned to keep the body within the predetermined temperature limits.

FIO Planning Project as a System

An FIO planning project may appear to have absolutely no relationship to the system we call the human body, but there are certain similarities. In the example of the human body, a series of processes including decision making (decider), analysis of input (input analyzer), checking the state of the system (monitoring device), and the purpose and process of the system (life) were discussed. If the FIO planning project fits the definition of a system and maintains the process described above, it could be said that the project is a system. The project as presented here has components (task forces) that are constrained or guided toward achieving the objectives of the system, which are to plan an FIO model. The project does fit the definition of a system, but does it perform the same processes as a system? The steering committee can be conceptualized as the decider because it makes decisions which guide the planning activities. The project obviously engages in a process that is the purpose for the existence of the system —to plan an FIO model. The identification of constraints, as presented in the last chapter, is similar to the process of analysis of input. The monitoring device is clearly the evaluation system suggested in Chapter 4 and explained in detail in Chapter 5. Based on this analysis, the FIO planning project can be considered a system or, minimally, has the potential of being a system.

The significance of conceptualizing the project as a system is that all natural systems, such as the human body, are basically systems that manage a process or, more correctly, a number of intricate processes. Further, they manage these processes with extreme effectiveness. The hypothesis that an FIO planning project which is designed and functions as a system would be exceedingly effective in producing an FIO model is certainly worth investigating.

A Systems-Management Model

Up to this point the processes involved in a system have been described, but processes are difficult to conceptualize. Therefore, to assist in the conceptualization of a system and its processes, a systems management model is depicted in Figure 1. At the lower level of the system is a box labeled "process" which has an arrow labeled "input" entering from the left and an arrow labeled "actual output" leaving from the right.

The box also includes the notation "planning FIO model," which refers to the primary function or purpose for the existence of the FIO project, that is, to plan an FIO model. The input into the system would include, among other things, any information about other FIO models, the competence levels of planning staff, their resources needed to function, problems raised by external sources, and the system constraints. The input into any system can be characterized as all the raw materials needed to produce the expected output, and any other factors or conditions that may affect the system or its operation. The line labeled "actual output" refers to the actual product of the system.

Directly above the box labeled "process" is a box labeled "decider," with the additional designation "steering committee." This indicates the role played by the steering committee. The point was made in the last chapter that the steering committee's major functions are to prepare overall planning strategies, determine planning policy, appoint and guide task forces, and assemble and approve final plans.

FIGURE 1

Management System for FIO Planning Project

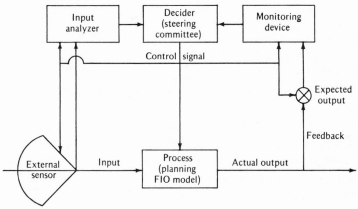

These functions in effect make the steering committee the manager or decider for the project. In actual practice, the steering committee would delegate many of its decision-making powers, as they relate to the solution of problems covered by planning policy and the interpretation and implementation of policy, to the project director.

The boxes to the right and left of the "decider" box are identified as "input analyzer" and "monitoring device." The fact that the decider was identified as the steering committee should not be interpreted to mean that these or any other boxes represent people. This is a process model and each box represents a process. The steering committee, responsible for the decisions affecting the total system, would assign individuals or a team the responsibility for performing the functions associated with the input analyzer and the monitoring device.

The input analyzer has the responsibility of screening all input to ascertain whether changes in input or new input have the potential of influencing the planning process or the FIO model being planned. The pie-shaped representation located below that of input analyzer and on the input line labeled "external sensor" is also part of the input-analyzer process. The shape of the external sensor was selected to symbolize an eye or radar device scanning the environment. If a system is to function effectively, it cannot depend on input alone but must be aware of factors in the environment that may become input and that could create problems. For example, a vicious smear campaign about FIO and the project may be spreading through the community. If it is not perceived and located by a scanning external sensor and acted on by a decider, the ultimate input may be a widely supported demand to discontinue the project. A less dramatic, but equally important, situation would be a change in the type of student entering the schools. "Sesame Street" is being heralded as having a significant impact on the basic knowledges and skills of pre-school children. If these claims are true, and early findings seem to indicate that they are, then many of the children entering school will require different types of learning experiences than the children who entered school in the pre–"Sesame Street" days. This is a trend that can be identified and compensated for in the planning of the FIO model long before countless children become disenchanted with school because the program is inadequate for their needs. The planners of an FIO model would obviously need this type of data if they are to plan effectively.

A monitoring device performs a function similar to that of an input analyzer except that it concentrates on the output end and the internal state of the system. The feedback line, leading from the actual output to expected output and eventually to a monitoring device, depicts a major function of the monitoring device. The actual output is compared with expected output to determine if the output leaving the system is acceptable within tolerable limits. *Expected output* is a systems term which refers to the performance requirements or mission objectives discussed in Chapter 3. Stated in other terms, it means that the FIO planning project was designed to prepare particular plans within a stated time. If the plans of a task force (actual output) are not consistent with the mission objectives and within the identified constraints (expected output), then a dysfunction exists in the system, and this becomes negative feedback which is relayed to the decider for resolution. Further, the monitoring device maintains a constant check on the state of the system. In an FIO planning project this would require an awareness of such factors as available resources, the membership of task forces, the progress being made by the task forces, and the competencies of all school personnel.

The functions performed by both input analyzer and

monitoring device require, as can be seen by the examples preceding, the acquisition, analysis, and storing of large amounts of information. The names *input analyzer* and *monitoring device,* although they have a mechanical ring, were selected because these processes could potentially be performed by a computer, which has enormous analytic, storage, and retrieval potential. A requisite for effective decision making is having the appropriate information available at the right time.

The only element of the systems-management model which has not been discussed are the many lines and arrows. The discussion to this point has implied that the lines had something to do with the transmitting of information. That is precisely what they represent. They can be viewed as communication lines which indicate the routing of information throughout the system. The model indicates that the steering committee receives information from both the input and output ends of the system to use in making decisions. The decisions deal with problems entering or found within the system which require solution. The lines labeled "control signal" are the lines along which solutions are transmitted. The solutions or directions are normally adjustments which are required to keep the system functioning at maximum efficiency. When the decider receives information which indicates that either the input is changing or the output is not acceptable, solutions or adjustments are decided on to compensate for the dysfunctions in the process. The control-signal lines to all other components also represent solutions for dysfunction in any of the components. In the case of expected output, this refers to the identification of objectives or performance requirements which may no longer be appropriate or acceptable and require revision.

A particular feature of the communication lines is that a communication loop exists between decider-steering committee and all other components of the system. This communication loop is referred to as a feedback system, or more correctly, the process is called cybernetics. The term *cybernetics* is derived from the Greek word, *kybernētēs,* which means "steersman" and thus alludes to the principal of feedback control. In general, the term *feedback* refers to a kind of reciprocal interaction between two or more actions in which one activity generates a second activity, which in turn redirects the first activity. The feedback control system incorporates three primary functions: (1) It generates movement of a system toward a goal or along a given path; (2) it compares the actual course of the system with its preplanned course and detects errors; and (3) it utilizes the error signal to redirect the system. The automatic pilot on modern aircraft, a missile programmed to hit a particular target, or a thermostatically controlled home heating system are typical examples of the application of cybernetic principles. The preceding discussion dealing with identification of problems, finding solutions, and control signal is also an example of the application of cybernetic principles.

The suggestion has been made that the steering committee could not be expected to carry on all the planning for a project of this size, and that task forces would be needed to plan the various components of the model. Figure 2 illustrates the relationship between the steering committee and each of the task forces. For purposes of illustration, three task forces are included in the model, but obviously more task forces will be needed. The inclusion of additional task forces would have complicated the model without increasing understanding, because any additional task forces would maintain the same relationship to the steering committee and the total process.

This representation was accomplished by a hypothetical explication of part of the "process" box in Figure 1. The total

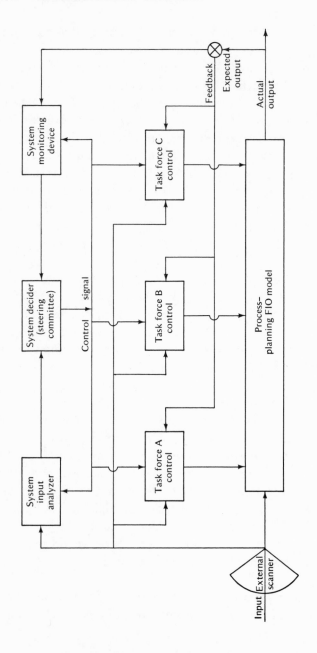

FIGURE 2
Total Management System for FIO Planning Project with Three Subsystems

process includes management and planning. In Figure 2, the management process of each of the task forces was explicated, but the planning process, as described in Chapter 3, remains in the "process" box at the bottom of the model. As now drawn, the model illustrates the management relationships that exist between the task forces and the steering committee. The model also indicates that the steering committee is not directly involved in the planning process. It plays a purely managerial role despite the fact that members of the steering committee will probably also be members of the various task forces. Of course, the model could be redrawn to give the steering committee a planning responsibility.

Each of the task forces, as depicted in Figure 2, is a subsystem of the total system, but these are also systems in their own right. As such they function precisely like the total system described in Figure 1. The only new element added to this model is the use of the term *control* in each of the task-force boxes. The single box labeled "control" for each task force is used to keep the model as uncluttered as possible. Actually, each box labeled "control" contains a decider, an input analyzer, an external scanner, and a monitoring device, and they perform processes identical to those attributed to the management system in Figure 1.

An FIO planning project that utilizes the systems-management principles and processes described here should be capable of controlling a very complex project and producing a viable flexible instructional-organization model which can be implemented with relative ease. To accomplish this, the steering committee must take the time to design a suitable management system, establish system procedures, and provide the resources and guidance necessary to perform the needed functions.

SYSTEMATIC DECISION MAKING

Now that basic systems concepts have been presented and a management system capable of identifying problems or dysfunctions within the system has been discussed, the next step will be to provide suggestions and procedures for the resolution of problems as they arise. The problems to be solved in an FIO planning project would probably fall into two categories: those related to the design of flexible instructional organization and those related to the process of planning. In either case, they are problems that will require resolution by some decision-making process. Therefore, consideration will be given to the decision-making process and a system for problem solving or decision making, which are used interchangeably.

The Decision-Making Process

Decision making can be defined as a process or strategy for devising solutions to problems. The different concepts of decision making are apparent in the sequences presented in the literature; these range from 3 to 10 steps. The simplest and, therefore, the most general series of steps is offered by Herbert A. Simon:

> Decision making comprises three principal phases: finding occasions for making a decision; finding possible courses of actions; and choosing among courses of action.[1]

Stanley Young, on the other hand, conceptualizes decision making as a 10-step process.

1. Organizational objectives must be defined.
2. Someone must raise the problem of how these goals can be achieved.
3. The nature of the problem must be investigated.

[1] Herbert A. Simon, *The New Science of Management Decision,* New York: Harper & Row, 1960, p. 1.

4. There should be a search for alternative solutions.
5. After full evaluation, the best alternative is selected.
6. Organizational consensus must be achieved.
7. The solution must be authorized.
8. The solution must be implemented.
9. Nondecision-makers must be instructed in the use of the decision.
10. An audit must be conducted for evaluating the effectiveness of the decision.[2]

Each of these conceptions of decision making is viable but may not be appropriate for an FIO planning project. The project is unique in the sense that it is not a permanent organization. It is an ad hoc group organized to produce a flexible instructional-organization model and will be replaced by a permanent organization that will manage the implemented model. Consequently, a decision-making process more appropriate to the needs of the project will be proposed. Because the objective for the project is to produce a plan for an FIO model, the following steps for decision making are suggested:

1. Identification of the problem
2. Diagnosis of the problem
3. Search for alternative solutions
4. Selection of the best solution
5. Ratification of the solution
6. Authorization of the solution

The steps start with the assumption that the steering committee and task forces have defined their objectives. The need for stated objectives in a systems context are crucial because, as pointed out in the discussion of expected output, unachieved objectives are a source of problems within the system.

[2] Stanley Young, *Management: A Systems Analysis*, Glenview, Ill.: Scott Foresman, 1966, p. 32.

Decision-Making Model

A decision-making model is a guide which illustrates how a decision is made within a given organization. Not all such models are the same. Each organization must design a model which satisfies its particular needs. While designing an appropriate model is important, it may be equally, if not more important, that the model be made available to all the personnel associated with the FIO project. Unless they are aware of and understand the methods and procedures to be used in decision making, they may generate more problems than they solve.

As a preface to a discussion of the process portrayed in Figure 3, a few words about the model should prove helpful. At the left of the model, the input line indicates that the inputs to this system are problems and the outputs, at the right, are solutions. The numbers and terms across the top of the model designate the steps in the decision-making process presented earlier, and the boxes in each of the columns labeled "steering committee" and "task force A (B, C)" indicate the involvement of each of the problem-solving groups at each step. The diamond-shaped symbols labeled "and"-"or" are called decision points and represent the need for a decision to send the problem to an individual component, all components, or a combination of components.

A break with the pattern set in the other models is that in this model the steering committee does not perform the decider function. In this case, the project director is assigned this responsibility; however, this arrangement is not mandatory, because the steering committee could serve as decider. Either of these situations is acceptable. To assist in making the choice, the following factors should be considered. The decision-making system presented here is designed to assist in solving problems for an organization whose primary function is the solution of a problem—planning an FIO model.

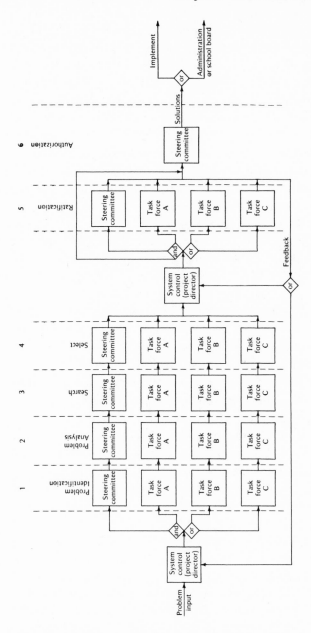

FIGURE 3
Decision-Making Model

In this case, two types of problems will require decisions: those related to planning the model and those that arise within the planning organization. The typical organization, such as a school district, has components that are assigned the responsibility of solving organizational problems so that decider is not usually involved in the process of solving these problems. An FIO planning project does not have components to solve organizational problems. Therefore, the choice is between having the project director serve as the control unit for the project with the steering committee serving as a problem solver, which is the case in Figure 3, or having the steering committee act as the control unit and appoint other groups to solve organizational problems. If the latter situation is selected, the model would have to be re-labeled. Either approach is viable, but the first alternative is more practical, because the project would have limited personnel resources.

Problem Identification (Step 1)

Prior to being assigned to the various problem-solving components, each problem has gone through a series of steps which should be understood by the problem solvers and the project director who will be managing the decision-making process. Each problem has an origin, but to be solved it must be brought to the attention of system control—the project director. Fortunately, within any system many potential problem raisers exist. In an FIO project, the input analyzer and the monitoring device are obvious sources, but others might include members of the board of education, central office staff, instructional staff, project staff, parents, and students. Although such a policy may appear masochistic, problem raisers should be encouraged to submit problems to the project director. The benefits to be gained by soliciting problems include the development of a feeling that everyone is being heard and the possibility that important but unrecognized problems will be raised.

As indicated in Figure 3, all problems become input into the system by being submitted to the system-control component. The project director is responsible for integrating and coordinating the decision-making process by screening, routing, scheduling, assigning, coordinating, expediting, and following up organizational problems. Each problem, as it enters the system, is screened to determine if it is a legitimate problem. Obviously, many of the problems raised may be capricious, insincere, or based on rumor. A problem of this sort would be returned to the sender with a note or letter explaining why it cannot be considered, or describing the actual situation. The problem may be returned to the problem raiser for several reasons. First, the problem may be trivial, which usually means that, while it is a legitimate problem, the time and effort to solve the problem would be disproportionate to the benefits to be derived from its solution. Second, the problem may be returned to the sender because the problem was not clearly stated or sufficient detail was not provided so that a decision could be made. Third, the problem raiser may be informed that the problem has been previously raised and is presently being worked on.

The legitimate problems remain in the system and a decision is made as to which is the appropriate group or combination of groups that should be able to produce a satisfactory solution. An especially important decision to be made at this point is the allocation of time and resources to solve the problem. At times there may be more problems entering the system than can reasonably be handled. To prevent an overload of the system, each problem, as it enters the system, is assigned a priority and is placed in a queue or waiting line.

Problems are then fed into the system at a rate that will insure an orderly and even flow of problems through the system.

The problems that are assigned to a particular problem-solving group have been screened and clarified, but the legitimacy of each problem must be determined. Therefore, before the problem is started through the decision-making process, it should be screened again, using the same techniques as system control. When a problem is established as legitimate, the first step in the decision-making process begins.

Problem identification, as has been suggested, is not one of the average educator's more highly developed skills. The prerequisite of successful problem identification is to be able to distinguish between a problem and nonproblem. A problem, in this instance, can be defined as any factor, situation, or condition which prevents or hinders the achievement of the objectives relative to planning a viable FIO model, or any conditions that necessitate a change in the objectives of the project or model. The criteria set forth in this definition would be used to determine whether a problem is a true problem. Problems associated with the stated objectives for the project or model do not have to be measured by a strict set of criteria. Any questions about the objectives or lack of objectives may be considered appropriate for acceptance as input into the decision-making system.

Problem Diagnosis (Step 2)

Problem diagnosis involves a thorough investigation to determine probable cause or causes. The investigation might begin by communication with the problem raiser to obtain as much information as possible. Problems identified by the input analyzer or the monitoring device would normally be accompanied by relevant data which would assist in ascertaining the probable cause or causes. The investigation should be as thorough as possible; for unless the most probable causes are found, an effective solution will not be forthcoming. On some occasions it may be discovered that a related problem must be solved before the problem under investigation can be resolved. In that case, a solution for the newly discovered problem would be sought before work could begin on the original problem.

Search for Alternative Solutions (Step 3)

Following the diagnosis of the problem and identification of probable causes comes the search for alternatives. Of all the steps in the decision-making process this is probably the least structured, because all the possible alternatives are not known. The creativity of the people involved in the decision-making process will certainly affect the alternatives that will be proposed. However, the resources made available to the problem solvers will also affect the number and quality of alternatives. Some possible sources would include past experience, research findings, experiences of other school districts, outside consultants, staff consultants, and national organizations.

This and the next step are similar to steps 5, 6, 12 and 13 in the systems-planning model discussed in the last chapter. Therefore, the simple statement that a forecast of cost-effectiveness ratio should be prepared for each of the alternatives should be adequate.

Selection of the Best Alternative (Step 4)

Since the procedures for selecting the best alternative were discussed thoroughly in Chapter 3, a lengthy explanation will not be repeated here. Suffice it to say that the objective is to select the alternative which promises the most benefit for the least cost in money, time, or effort.

Ratification of the Solution (Step 5)

Following the selection of the best alternative, the solution is returned to the project director for routing through the appropriate task forces for ratification. Upon receipt of the solution, the project director sends it to the task forces whose work may be affected by the solution for their ratification, or to the next step if ratification is not needed. Ratification does not imply the power to accept or reject the solution. The task forces receiving a solution for ratification will carefully consider the effect that the solution may have on their planning. Three conclusions appear possible: (1) It will have no effect; (2) it will have an effect, but compensatory action is possible; and (3) it will have a serious effect, and no compensatory action appears possible. If all the task forces affected by the solution indicate that either of the first two conclusions is the situation, then no problem exists, and the solution may proceed to the next step. However, if any task force or combination of task forces indicate that the third condition exists, there obviously is a conflict which must be resolved. The conflict can be resolved by either asking the task force to reconsider its solution in the light of the constraints identified by the other task forces or having the task forces caucus to see if they can resolve the problem.

The ratification process serves two important organizational functions. The first and most obvious is that, in the process of examining the proposed solution, flaws or weaknesses which had escaped notice may be brought to light and corrected before the solution is implemented. The second benefit to be gained by this procedure is promotion of coordination of effort between the task forces. One of the most commonly cited characteristics of organizations is that they promote coordination of effort among their members. The coordination of effort in an FIO planning project will depend upon the staff of the project perceiving their actions as contributing to the goals of the project. The more difficult it is for the staff to perceive the relationship between their work and the total project, the more difficult coordination becomes. Therefore, the involvement of staff members in the assessment and ratification of solutions should contribute to their perceiving the relationship between their efforts and those of other staff members. Not only will they become aware of what others are doing, but they also will gain some satisfaction from knowing that their opinions were solicited and considered.

Authorization (Step 6)

The authorization of solutions may be a very routine matter or very troublesome, depending on the delegation and definition of authority and the effectiveness of the problem solvers in producing valid and viable solutions. The delegation and definition of authority for authorizing solutions must be defined as explicitly as possible to insure that authorizations are legitimate and will not be challenged. For an FIO planning project, the steering committee should have the power to authorize any decisions related to the FIO model being developed. Their authorization is limited to the extent that the final model must be approved by the board of education. Hence, their authorization actually means that they have authorized the solution for inclusion in the model and eventual recommendation to the board of education that the model be authorized as submitted.

Solutions applicable to the management or operations of the project are another matter. Every effort should be made to define the conditions under which the steering committee is authorized to approve a particular action, and those situations in which its power is limited to recommending a solution for authorization by the superintendent or board of education. For example, decisions involving the expenditure of money or the use of physical facilities would probably have to be authorized by the superintendent or school board, but the decision to appoint a task force or to schedule meetings would be authorized by the steering committee.

In the delegation of authority, the state laws governing education must be considered; but beyond the laws, the board of education, with the guidance of the steering committee and the administrative staff, would have final authority. The question of who will authorize what solutions must be answered by each school district. The important point is that everyone associated with the project is aware of who has the authority to authorize which solutions. Then, assuming that the decision makers are performing their functions effectively, authorization would become a rather routine matter.

At the output end of the model in Figure 3, solutions arrive at a decision point. The project director must decide whether the solution may be implemented or submitted to the superintendent or school board for final authorization. A statement of policies and procedures regarding the delegation of authority and authorization power would guide the project director in making this decision.

SUMMARY

The management of an FIO planning project can be most difficult due to the amount and scope of planning required. In this chapter, the emphasis has been on methods and procedures for managing an FIO project. To assist in conceptualizing the management process, it was suggested that the project be viewed as a system. A system was defined as a set of components organized in such a way as to constrain or guide action toward the accomplishment of the purposes for which it exists. To accomplish its functions, a living system has certain characteristics; these include:

1. A process or processes
2. Input and output
3. A decider
4. An input analyzer
5. A monitoring device

Each of these characteristics was explained and application was made to a systems-management model for an FIO project. The point was made that this was a process model and, therefore, the characteristics attributed to a system were actually processes. The functions needed to perform the processes were discussed and suggestions were made concerning the person or persons who might perform these functions.

The point also was made that the primary function of the steering committee is to manage the decision-making or problem-solving process for the project. To accomplish this, the steering committee must decide on a problem-solving process and design a decision-making system. Although many problem solving model exist, a 6-step model was suggested. It includes:

1. Identification of the problem
2. Diagnosis of the problem
3. Search for alternative solutions
4. Selection of the best solution
5. Ratification of the solution
6. Authorization of the solution

Using this model, a decision-making model was developed and explained. The recommendation was made that the project director serve as control or manager of the decision-making system. The project director would be responsible for integrating and coordinating the decision-making process by screening, routing, scheduling, assigning, coordinating, expediting, and following up organizational problems. Finally, each step in the decision-making process was discussed and suggestions were provided to assist the decision makers.

SELECTED BIBLIOGRAPHY

Bross, Irwin D. *Design for Decisions.* New York: Macmillan (1953).

Feyereisen, Kathryn V., A. John Fiorino, and Arlene T. Nowak. *Supervision and Curriculum Renewal: A Systems Approach.* New York: Appleton (1970).

Neuschel, Richard F. *Management by System.* New York: McGraw-Hill (1963).

Simon, Herbert A. *The New Science of Management Decision.* New York: Harper & Row (1960).

Young, Stanley. *Management: A Systems Analysis.* Glenview, Ill.: Scott, Foresman (1966).

Planning
for Evaluation

Evaluation is a term so widely used that many people assume that all other people define it precisely as they do. Unfortunately, this notion is as inaccurate as the assumption that any group of Americans would agree on the definition of democrarcy. In education, evaluation has been used to refer to everything from a standardized paper-and-pencil test to a visceral judgment based on subjective evidence. There is obviously a great deal of confusion surrounding the concept of evaluation. This is partially due to the use of *measurement* and *evaluation* by educators as interchangeable terms. Actually, the terms have separate and distinct meanings.

EVALUATION AND MEASUREMENT

Educational measurement is normally considered a process that attempts to quantify the degree to which a particular trait has been acquired by a student. The most common instrument used in measurement is the paper-and-pencil test. Fundamentally, the measurement process is descriptive. It attempts to describe, in numerical rather than verbal terms, the degree to which an individual or group possesses a particular trait. In measurement, one tends to concentrate on specific types of traits and attempts to measure these traits as precisely as possible. The tests and processes used in educational measurement are analogous to the test borings at a building site prior to excavation. The purpose of the test borings is to determine the nature of the subsoils and the depth of bedrock. The various subsoils are measured to determine density, weight-bearing ability, and water-retention ability. Although each of the measurements is precise and many test borings are made, the engineers do not have a total picture of the subsoils. At best they have a good sample, but they do not know the true nature of the area until the hole has been dug. Educational measurement is very similar. Each test given to a child or group of children amounts to a test boring in the field of knowledge, skills, or attitudes being measured. Hopefully, these measurements are accurate; but, at best, they give only a partial view of the total area. As a consequence of this partial view, evaluation becomes necessary.

The process of evaluation begins where measurement ends. Evaluation utilizes the information derived from the measurement process, as well as from such other sources as self-rating scales, questionnaires, direct observation, and interviews, to make a value judgment or decision. Evaluation may be defined as *a systematic process for gathering information necessary to judge the adequacy of the achievement of the objectives of the system.* There are four important aspects of this definition. First, evaluation implies a *systematic process for gathering information,* which excludes casual, uncontrolled observations. Second, evaluation involves making *value judgments* or *decisions.* Third, evaluation always assumes that objectives *exist and are stated.* Without objectives, it is obviously impossible to judge or decide the extent to which the objectives have been achieved. Fourth, the term *system* refers to the *total system.* In an educational context, this includes curriculum, instruction, administration, supervision, buildings and grounds, lunch program, health program, and all other components which are part of the total school system. Therefore, each component must have objectives which serve as a basis for evaluation.

EVALUATION AND FEEDBACK

In recent years, a new dimension has been added to the concept of evaluation. The feedback or cybernetic principles discussed earlier have been wed to the traditional notions of evaluation. In education, this means that evaluative information is used for diagnostic purposes; that is, the degree of achievement is compared to stated objectives to determine whether the achievement is at acceptable levels. If achievement is below acceptable levels, this information becomes negative feedback and is used to redirect or adjust the system so that it is capable of achieving the objectives. For example, if the measurement and evaluation information about a reading program indicates that the students are not achieving at an acceptable level, the information is analyzed to determine the probable causes, so that adjustments can be made in the process, in order that the students will be able to achieve at acceptable levels. This same process would be utilized in each component of the school system.

EVALUATION IN A FLEXIBLE
INSTRUCTIONAL-ORGANIZATION CONTEXT

Any school district considering a move to FIO should place a high priority on establishing an evaluation and feedback system. As has been suggested throughout this text, a flexible instructional organization demands that extensive changes be made in a school system. The amount of change required will draw considerable public attention. While most educators would agree that the school's function as a public institution is not simply to keep the public satisfied, the fact must be faced that without public support, little can be accomplished by the school. Therefore, sufficient evaluative information will be needed to keep the public informed and, hopefully, allay the fears which accompany any significant change in the accepted way of doing things.

In the matter of planning and implementing a flexible instructional organization, evaluation becomes a crucial element. An evaluation of the existing program and procedures will assist in the identification of specific problems which must be solved by the new organization. Clearly, the possibility of developing a more effective model would be enhanced if potential problems are identified and compensated for in the new model. In addition, it may be discovered through this evaluation of the existing program and procedures that certain aspects of it can be utilized in the new model with little or no revision. The data gathered during the evaluation of the existing programs and procedures will serve as a bench mark for the analysis of data gathered after the model has been implemented. Lack of data about previous programs has been a serious weakness of many of the innovative programs adopted by schools. After the innovation has been adopted, the bench-mark data needed for a comparison of past and present practices is no longer available, except perhaps in the case of student achievement. Hence, schools which had not collected the necessary bench-mark data had no way of knowing if the benefits had been derived from the innovation they had adopted. Precautions should be taken by any school planning staff differentiation to obviate the possibility of finding themselves in this awkward position.

The new relationships, ways of working, and programs inherent in a flexible instructional organization will require new methods for determining effectiveness. As suggested earlier, student achievement, while important, is not the only basis for evaluating an innovation. Some of the benefits to be derived from the new organization are in the more humane utilization and treatment of the staff and students. While this point will be discussed later in this chapter, it is mentioned here to emphasize the need for the development of an evaluation and feedback system which is capable of making evaluative judgments in this affective area.

In addition, any innovation which will so radically change a school system will doubtlessly contain numerous "bugs." It is virtually impossible for any group planning a flexible instructional organization to plan for every contingency. If this assumption is correct, and there is every reason to believe that it is, then the need for an evaluation and feedback system is incontestable. The new organization must be capable of identifying any dysfunctions and feeding this information back into the systems so that appropriate remedial action can be taken. To exclude this capability will either cause the organization's eventual collapse or limit severely its capability of achieving its full potential.

EVALUATION TASK FORCE

The foregoing discussion was presented to establish the rationale for setting up an effective evaluation and feedback system. The obvious question now is What can a school district do to avoid the potential pitfalls in the evaluation area? The most rational answer to this question is to establish an evaluation task force as early as feasible during the initial-planning stages of the project. Since these people must carry on two functions almost simultaneously, they should be provided as much lead time as possible to accomplish their work. They will be responsible for gathering the bench-mark data necessary for later comparison with the new data derived from the new organization, and for designing the feedback system for the new organization.

The membership of this task force should include both highly specialized personnel and people who will be affected by the evaluation or utilize the information for decision-making purposes. This list might include

1. A test-and-measurement specialist who can assist in selecting or devising the appropriate data-gathering instruments
2. Teachers representing various levels and subject-matter areas who can contribute their expertise in the areas or in program and personnel matters
3. Administrative personnel who can assist in the administrative-procedures area and in identifying budget and board-policy limits
4. Students who may provide insights into student concerns
5. Lay people who can provide insights into parent and community concerns and desires
6. Evaluation-specialist consultant to be made available to the task force on a regular basis (perhaps monthly after initial orientation period)

The personnel listed here should not be considered mandatory. Each school district must decide on its own mix of personnel, but the test-and-measurement and evaluation specialists are highly desirable. A test-and-measurement specialist usually can be found in guidance departments. The evaluation specialist will, in all likelihood, have to be brought in from the outside. Colleges, universities, state departments of education, or testing agencies are the most likely sources for the evaluation specialist. As a point of information, the test-and-measurement and evaluation fields are distinctly different specialties. The test-and-measurement specialist's expertise is in his knowledge of various types of standardized tests and his ability to devise instruments to measure various traits or conditions. On the other hand, the evaluation specialist is an expert in designing total evaluation programs, devising methods for effectively utilizing evaluative information, devising monitoring schedules, and similar types of activities.

MISSION PROFILE FOR EVALUATION TASK FORCE

The remainder of this chapter will be devoted to a discussion of the various tasks to be performed by the evaluation task force. To assist in the conceptualization of the total process of planning an evaluation and feedback system, Figure 4 presents the major steps to be taken and the sequence in which they might occur. In keeping with the approach used in this text, a word must be said about following a cookbook approach. The mission profile outlined in Figure 4 is purely

FIGURE 4
Mission Profile for Evaluation Task Force

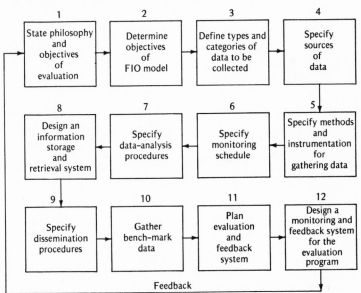

suggestive. Each evaluation task force should prepare its own mission profile. This obviously does not mean that the mission profile presented here should be disregarded. Rather, it should be perceived as a guide which must be developed further to take into account local needs, conditions, and resources.

Step 1: State philosophy and objectives of evaluation. The task force should prepare a statement defining evaluation and how it will be used in the new FIO model. The overall objective for the evaluation and feedback system might be to provide the appropriate information to the appropriate personnel at the appropriate time to permit the most effective decision making to occur. This objective could be expressed in other terms and expanded upon to provide a statement of specific objectives. In addition, a statement of policies should be prepared. The statement may include policies such as the following:

1. An open evaluation program will be maintained at all times.
2. Any person to be evaluated will be provided an opportunity to have input into the planning of the evaluation.
3. All persons being evaluated will be made aware that they are being evaluated.
4. All persons being evaluated will be informed of the criteria to be used to evaluate them.
5. The results of evaluation, except those of a personal nature, will be made available to all interested parties.
6. The results of personal evaluation will be made available to the person being evaluated.

Step 2: Determine objectives of the FIO model. The evaluation task force should be involved in determining the objectives of the total flexible instructional-organization model. Their involvement can contribute to the success of the total project in two ways. First, the success of an evaluation program is contingent on a thorough knowledge of the objectives. By participating in the determination of the objectives, the task force members will gain a first-hand knowledge of the objectives and the rationale behind each. Second, members of the evaluation task force should be able to assist in stating the objectives in terms which will facilitate the evaluation process.

Educators are familiar with curricular and instructional objectives, so little will be said here about these types of objectives. Our primary concern in this chapter is with objectives for the model being developed. Objectives should be stated for the various levels of the organization and would include total organization, each component, and each position. To assist in the preparation of these objectives, the following suggestions and views may prove helpful. (1) *Total organization:* It goes without saying that the purpose of a school is to educate children, but for a modern school organization, this will not suffice. Many things happen in a school in addition to educating children. It is a society and way of life which occupies a major part of the lives of the members of this society or organization. As such, the organization has a responsibility to promote the welfare of the membership. All participants should derive some benefits, aside from salary, from their association with the organization. To this end, the organization should contribute to the fulfillment of each member, including students. This would include a sense of belonging, self-worth, acceptance, achievement, support, adequacy, and self-actualization. Some readers may be repelled by this conceptualization of the functions of an organization. However, when considered in the context of staffing differentiation and a flexible instructional organization, this concept may not seem out of place. One of the basic reasons for moving to FIO is to provide a more suitable environment for enhancing and providing for the differences found in students and staff. Logically, then, stating objectives for the total organization which specify the benefits to be derived by the members would be consistent with the rationale for differentiated staffing. (2) *Component objectives:* Each component of the total school system should have a statement of objectives which specifies, as precisely as possible, the functions and tasks for which it is responsible. Personnel in curriculum and instruction, administration, supervision, guidance, health, buildings and grounds, and all other functional components should prepare a statement of objectives for approval by the steering committee. The reason for steering-committee approval is to protect against duplication and voids. Since the steering committee would be responsible for overall coordination of the planning project, they would be in the best position to perform this task. (3) *Position objectives:* The objectives for each position may be stated as objectives or as the functions and tasks to be performed by the individual occupying each position. Ideally, the functions and tasks should be as specific as possible to provide a basis for evaluating the effectiveness of each staff member. Very few school districts have attempted to state specific tasks and functions for staff members. Consequently, evaluation has proven most difficult. A perennial problem in most school districts is evaluating teachers and administrators. If one factor could be isolated as the cause of this problem, it would probably be a lack of an adequate description of the functions and tasks of a competent teacher or administrator. Clearly, this problem can be avoided if a specific statement of functions and tasks or objectives for each position is prepared.

Before the next step is discussed, a few words should be said concerning the method used for stating organizational objectives. The standard practice for stating objectives has been to describe terminal behavior, the ultimate goal, or the ideal. While this procedure is widely accepted and appropriate for some situations, it has within it a built-in frustration factor. Schools have stated the objective of having all children reading at grade level. Although this is a desirable objective, the chances of achieving it are remote. A more reasonable approach would be to state yearly goals. For example, the goal in reading for the coming year might be to increase the number of students reading at grade level or above by 5 percent. Other examples would be to:

1. Reduce student absences by 5 percent
2. Increase library usage by 5 percent
3. Reduce teacher turnover by 3 percent
4. Reduce vandalism by 10 percent

Stating objectives in this manner increases the chances of achieving them, and can provide motivation for further improvement.

Step 3: Define types and categories of data to be collected. The objectives, which would be completed at this point in the planning process, should provide a basis for determining the types of data needed to carry on an effective evaluation program. Therefore, no effort will be made here to present an exhaustive exposition of types or categories of data. The information provided here will attempt to highlight some dimensions of education and the educative process which have not been a part of traditional evaluation programs.

Cost effectiveness is one area which has been neglected in education. A change from traditional staffing patterns to flexible instructional organization will raise many questions concerning cost. Obviously then, a school district would be acting wisely if it anticipated the questions and prepared itself to collect data which could be used to determine cost effectiveness. For some readers, this may be interpreted to mean that PPBS (planning, programming, budgeting system) is being recommended. Any school district planning for flexible instructional organization should probably avoid PPBS until their new model had been implemented, but a more informal system could be used. The cost of programs could be determined by adding the cost of salaries and supplies rather than the more precise method required by PPBS. The function of this data is to provide a comparison between the cost of the new and the old organizations. Some school districts have discovered that they could provide more educational opportunities for students by making more electives available or that they could increase the number of adults available to a given group of students with no increase in cost.

Student evaluation is an accepted practice in all school districts, but, traditionally, it has been restricted to achievement. Unfortunately, efforts to demonstrate that an innovation has raised the student's achievement level significantly have usually concluded that there was no significant difference between the new and old. This is probably caused by the high performance level of our students. Few nations can claim as high an educational level for their total population as we can. The result is that extreme efforts are needed to cause a significant gain in student achievement. Consequently, a school district planning a change to flexible instructional organization cannot promise, nor expect, exceptional gains in student achievement. Since this is a predictable phenomenon, educators should not be overly concerned. This is not to suggest that flexible instruction organization will not contribute to raising the achievement level of students. It probably will, but the slight gain may not provide an adequate basis for justifying the effort involved in moving to flexible instructional organization. To evaluate the new organization, other types of data will be needed. The sources for this data will be found in the reasons for moving to the new organization. Certainly, each school district must identify its own reasons, but the typical reasons given would include more appropriate teaching-learning strategies for individual students, expanded educational opportunities, and programs to satisfy individual needs. Evaluation of whether or not the new organization is providing these benefits is a difficult, but not impossible, task.

It seems reasonable to assume that the attitudes and behaviors of students will improve if they are receiving the benefits ascribed to the new organization. Therefore, the needed data can be obtained in three ways. (1) A standardized or locally prepared attitude inventory can be utilized to determine the students' attitude toward school, learning, program, instruction, and the like. (2) The attitudes of students toward the school and the educative process can be determined by the behaviors they demonstrate. An improved attitude toward school would probably result in:

1. Decrease in the number of excused absences
2. Decrease in the number of cases of tardiness
3. Greater use in the library
4. Fewer discipline problems
5. Decrease in the dropout rate
6. Decline in vandalism
7. Fewer teacher complaints about students
8. Decline in referral of discipline problems to the administration or guidance personnel

(3) A follow-up study of graduates could be used to determine the percentage of students seeking additional education, success in obtaining employment, and satisfaction with the preparation they received.

Traditionally, teacher evaluation has been a part of all school systems, but it has tended to be unidimensional and somewhat less than effective. The criteria used for evaluating teachers, such as appearance, are hardly defensible as a basis for determining effectiveness. The use of student achievement as a criterion for determining effectiveness also suffers from serious flaws. The primary flaw is that student achievement may not measure effectiveness of instruction. High achievement levels of a particular group of students may be the result of their high intelligence rather than teacher effectiveness. To overcome this problem, other measures are needed. Measurement of output lacks significance unless the input is also known. This means that a pretest-posttest procedure must be used. Students should be tested before they begin a particular educational experience and after they have completed the experience. In this way, the amount of progress made by the students can be determined. More reliable evaluation of effectiveness can then be made by comparing actual progress with the progress that could normally be expected from the students. Obviously, the brightest students should achieve at the highest levels and average students should demonstrate average achievement. But, when average students achieve at higher-than-average levels, the conclusion can be drawn that more effective teaching had occurred.

As was suggested in the discussion of student evaluation, a change to a flexible instructional organization should provide certain benefits for teachers which would change attitudes and behaviors. Some of the techniques suggested for evaluating the flexible instructional organization can be used in the teacher and staff component of the system. A standardized or locally produced attitude inventory can be used to determine teacher satisfaction with:

1. Curriculum
2. Teaching-learning strategies
3. Schedule for instruction
4. Peer relationships
5. Administrative relationships
6. Help received in solving instructional problems

7. Assistance in interpreting curriculum
8. Their role in the decision-making process

The behaviors of teachers that may provide clues as to an improvement in attitude might include

1. Decrease in sickness or personal-business absences
2. Fewer cases of tardiness
3. Fewer complaints about working conditions
4. Requests for transfer into experimental schools
5. Fewer than normal requests for transfer out of experimental schools
6. Increase in the number of teacher-initiated innovations

The types of information suggested preceding are all aimed at providing feedback data for the new organization. In addition, the data will provide an excellent basis for comparing the old instructional organization and the new FIO.

Step 4: Specify sources of data.   Although several sources for data were identified in step 3, in a feedback-system context, many other sources for data can be tapped. Aside from students and staff, some of these sources might include:

1. Employers of graduates
2. Parents
3. Colleges that graduates attend
4. Taxpayers
5. Social agencies which serve youth

Other sources would depend on the types of data specified in step 3.

At the conclusion of step 4, the evaluation task force should be able to specify rather precisely the types of data they will gather and the sources they will use for obtaining the data.

Step 5: Specify methods and instrumentation for gathering data.   At this step, the services of a test-and-measurement specialist would prove invaluable. His knowledge of commercially produced instruments and skill in developing instruments would contribute greatly to performing this task. The importance of effectively accomplishing this task cannot be overemphasized. The reliability and validity of the data collected will be determined by the methods and instruments used. Therefore, great care must be taken during this step to insure that the data will serve the purpose for which they are collected.

One method of obtaining data, which is often overlooked, is an analysis of the regularly kept records of the school. The budget records, personnel records, attendance records, guidance records, and cumulative records of students are all excellent sources for the types of data mentioned in step 3. The other predominant method includes various types of instruments such as rating scales, attitude inventories, questionnaires, interview inventories, and objective tests.

When a decision is made concerning the method or type of instrument to be used to collect a particular set of data, the decision must be made whether to purchase or produce the instrument. A general rule might be adopted to purchase commercially produced instruments whenever possible, that is, assuming they are appropriate for the task. The rationale behind this rule is that, generally speaking, the commercially produced instruments are designed by people with more expertise than can be found in the typical school district. An excellent source of information about commercially produced instruments is the series *The Mental Measurement Yearbooks,* prepared by Oscar Boros.[1]

Step 6: Specify monitoring schedule. One of the principal weaknesses of evaluation programs is that they are haphazard. Many school systems have the mistaken notion that a

---

[1] Oscar K. Boros, *The Mental Measurement Yearbooks,* Highland Park, N.J.: The Gryphon Press.

variety of tests, with as few repetitions as possible, constitutes a desirable program. A variety of instruments produced by different publishers would generate incompatible results which might be useless for comparison purposes. A desirable and meaningful program would use comparable instruments over a period of years, with only such changes as are required by the obsolescence of the instruments or the publication of improved instruments.

The monitoring of learning, attitudes, and other processes should be scheduled on a regular basis. Extended periods between data-collection procedures can allow serious dysfunctions or situations to develop which could be extremely difficult to correct. The evaluation task force should prepare a monitoring schedule which will allow frequent measurements to be taken so that an effective evaluation can be made. Although frequent monitoring or testing has been criticized by both educators and laymen, much of the criticism can be overcome by a carefully conceived schedule which causes a minimum disruption of the normal routine and utilizes resoures other than the teacher for the mechanics of correcting and recording scores. Furthermore, frequent monitoring can be justified to critics by taking the position that the alternative to frequent monitoring is ignorance. Since effective decision making and problem solving depends on the availability of appropriate information, the monitoring schedule must be designed to produce the information.

Step 7: Specify data-analysis procedures. The nature of the evaluation and feedback system for an FIO model will require relatively unsophisticated analysis procedures. Elementary statistical analysis will probably suffice; but, in some instances, more sophisticated analysis may be desirable. Consequently, careful thought should be given to how data will be analyzed. A research specialist might prove to be a valuable resource while these deliberations are being conducted.

Step 8: Design information storage and retrieval system. The type of evaluation and feedback system being proposed here can generate enormous amounts of information. The possibility exists that the total system may be overloaded with information and breakdown. The need for an effective information storage and retrieval system seems evident. A school district with computer capabilities should have a relatively easy task of designing a very adequate system. School districts without computer capabilities will have to be more creative in approaching this problem. One method for solving this problem might be to maintain a 3-step filing system. The master file would contain all data collected, including copies of all instruments used in the monitoring process. The next level of files would contain summaries of the information gathered through the administration of the various instruments and other techniques. The third level files would contain an abstract of all the summaries covering a period of years. Using this system, a person seeking information would start at the third-level files. If additional information is needed, the location of specific information in the second-level file would be provided by the entries in the third-level file. The same precedure would be followed if the original documents were needed.

Regardless of the method used, the paramount objective is to design an information storage and retrieval system that will provide the appropriate information when it is needed. The importance of this capability might well require the utilization of an expert. The money spent would return untold dividends for the decision makers within the school district.

Step 9: Specify dissemination procedures. The evaluation task force must make three decisions at this step. First, they must specify the recipients of the various types of information generated by the evaluation and feedback system.

Second, they should determine the format to be used for disseminating. Care must be taken to insure that the format will expedite rather than hinder communication. Third, they should prepare a reporting schedule to guide the staff responsible for preparing the information and to assist in supplying the necessary information at the appropriate time to facilitate decision making.

Step 10: Gather bench-mark data. At the conclusion of step 9, the evaluation task force will be in a position to gather the bench-mark data needed for later comparison with the data collected following the implementation of FIO. A question which must be resolved at this step is whether the evaluation task force will gather and evaluate the data or whether an outside group should be hired to perform this task. Some educators advocate the utilization of external resources during the initial stages of planning and implementation. The rationale behind this position is that members of the local school staff may be unduly influenced by their desire to have the project succeed. Furthermore, an evaluation conducted by outside consultants may have greater credibility in the eyes of the general public. In view of the possible opposition to or apprehension about the move to FIO, having the evaluation conducted by an outside group may be a worthwhile investment. The professional staff might also feel more comfortable in the knowledge that they will not be accused of introducing a bias into the results of the evaluation. Should a school district decide to employ external evaluators, they should be brought in early in the planning process and used as consultants for the evaluation task force.

Step 11: Plan evaluation and feedback component. The functions to be performed by the evaluation and feedback system will require the establishment of an evaluation and feedback component or department. There is no set organizational pattern for accomplishing this task. School districts with a research and development team may utilize the team, but school districts without this capability must plan their own component. Step 11 involves specifying:

1. The number and types of personnel needed
2. The professional and personal qualifications needed for each position
3. The types of relationship between the members of the component
4. The relationship between the evaluation component and other components in the school district
5. The functions and tasks to be performed by each member of the component
6. A budget for the component

Step 12: Design a monitoring and feedback system for the evaluation program. To insure that the evaluation program and evaluation component remain relevant, a monitoring and feedback system should be designed for both the program and component. Therefore, the evaluation task force should design a monitoring and feedback system capable of identifying dysfunctions within the evaluation component.

The steps to be taken would be essentially the same as those outlined above, except that this time they would focus on the evaluation and feedback system and the evaluation component rather than the total FIO project.

Final Thoughts

The mission profile discussed earlier may seem to be an extremely tedious and perhaps unnecessarily detailed process. Before making a hasty judgment, the reader should consider the complexity of the total process of developing a system for landing a man on the moon. The very nature of the moon project allows the planner to identify and control the variable which might cause the project to fail. Educators are not quite so fortunate. The variables which may cause failure in an educational system are not only difficult to identify but also extremely difficult to control.

Consequently, educators engaged in planning complex projects must be prepared to devote considerable time and energy to detailed planning prior to implementation. Following implementation, most available time and energy will be spent attempting to insure success of the project. Few resources will be available to design an evaluation and feedback system.

SUMMARY

This chapter has been devoted to applying evaluation and feedback principles to a total FIO project. Measurement and evaluation were identified as two distinctly different processes. The feedback or cybernetic concept was presented as an integral part of any evaluation program. A case was presented for the establishment of an evaluation task force as early as possible in the total-project planning schedule. A mission profile for the evaluation task force was presented and discussed. It includes the following steps:

1. State philosophy and objectives of evaluation
2. Determine objectives of FIO model
3. Define types and categories of data to be collected
4. Specify sources of data
5. Specify methods and instrumentation for gathering data
6. Specify monitoring schedule
7. Specify data-analysis procedures
8. Design an information storage and retrieval system
9. Specify dissemination procedures
10. Gather bench-mark data
11. Plan evaluation and feedback component
12. Design a monitoring and feedback system for the evaluation program

SELECTED BIBLIOGRAPHY

Ahmann, J. Stanley and Marvin D. Glock. *Evaluating Pupil Growth: Principles of Tests and Measurement,* 3rd ed. Boston: Allyn & Bacon (1967).

Association for Supervision and Curriculum Development. *Evaluation as Feedback Guide.* Yearbook. Edited by Fred T. Wilhelms. Washington, D.C.: The Association (1967).

Barton, Allen H. *Organizational Measurement.* Princeton, N.J.: College Entrance Examination Board (1961).

Beatty, Walcott H. *Improving Educational Assessment & An Inventory of Measures of Affective Behavior.* Washintgon, D.C.: The Association for Supervision and Curriculum Development (1969).

Boros, Oscar K. *The Mental Measurement Yearbooks.* Highland Park, N.J.: The Gryphon Press.

Feyereisen, Kathryn V., A. John Fiorino, and Arlene T. Nowak. *Supervision and Curriculum Renewal: A Systems Approach.* New York: Appleton (1970).

Goodlad, John I., John F. O'Toole, and Louise L. Tyler. *Computers and Information Systems in Education.* New York: Harcourt Brace Jovanovich (1966).

Loughary, John W. *Man-Machine Systems in Education.* New York: Harper & Row (1966).

Wicks, John W. and Donald L. Beggs. *Evaluation for Decision-Making in the Schools.* Boston: Houghton Mifflin (1971).

Index

72 73 74 75 76   9 8 7 6 5 4 3 2 1